THE STORY OF MY LIFE

CHIEF MOODY 55

Steven D. Moody

THE STORY OF MY LIFE

Copyright © 2024 by STEVEN D. MOODY

All rights reserved. No part of this book may be reproduced or transmitted in any form or by any means without written permission from the author.

DEDICATION

Dedicated to all Emergency Responders and their families.

And to Rosie, the person who made it all possible.

CONTENTS

Dedication — iii

Foreword — vii

Introduction — 1

Chapter 1: Growing Up — 2

Chapter 2: My Career In Salina — 22

Chapter 3: My Career In Leavenworth — 73

Chapter 4: My Career In Stafford County — 95

Chapter 5: My Career In Eldorado — 133

Chapter 6: A Summary With An Ending — 151

Acknowledgement — 162

FOREWORD
SFD ICON'S WORTH KNOWING AND READING

By Tim Unruh

At some point in the spring of 1999, Steve Moody graced my professional life as a high-ranking member of the Salina Fire Department.

The introduction was pleasant, also imposing, as the tall burly fellow with a mustache and big smile, first greeted me in Fire Station 1.

I was new to Salina at the time, clamoring to learn the community, and gain acceptance from sources as a local newspaper reporter.

First impressions were clear as I sized up the man in uniform, consisting of dark slacks, polished black shoes, a white shirt and name tag pinned to his pocket.

Steve struck me as professional who loved his job as a firefighter, clearly dedicated to serving and protecting the community where he grew up; a happy man with a booming voice, enhanced by an enthusiastic laugh.

Early notes to self were "nice guy, clearly in command and in charge, especially if called into service; and it's probably not a good idea to tick him off."

Steve was, and still is, a friend of the news media, who embraced the special partnership with reporters and photographers as essential to his service.

It was a joy to visit him at the SFD, or chat over the phone.

That's about the sum total of my memories of the man, because he left the department and Salina in 2005.

I wish he could have stayed put, but fate had other ideas for Steve whose charm elevated him to hero status at home and in other communities he served.

His 38 years as a firefighter, paramedic, and respected leader, continued to glisten as he led fire departments — while filling other positions at times at Leavenworth, Stafford, and El Dorado — in that order.

The rest of this writing is courtesy of family, colleagues, friends and some classmates whose admiration of Steve runs deep.

Included with the honor of being asked to write this was learning more about Steve Moody, and the strength he demonstrated in overcoming a number of challenges. Please read on to learn more.

Among his tremendous experiences, and-or feats, included delivering a baby, Eva, in Stafford. He depicted the heroism in an awe shucks sort of way — calling it "just a grab & catch."

Accomplishments included directing Stafford County Emergency Management, Stafford County Emergency Medical Service, serving as fire chief, modernizing the department, and writing a blog.

As El Dorado's fire chief, Steve ran the department and worked closely with the state and federal prison systems.

"It's been a wonderful career," he said in a phone conversation in early January.

Steve left Salina mildly heartbroken for not being offered the fire chief position, but vowed not to hold a grudge, and bid farewell as a legend to many.

"He was great to work with," said Willis Sutton, of Manhattan, an SFD retiree who spent the bulk of his career in lockstep with the man who set a strong example.

As a co-worker and leader, Steve used his knowledge and experience — having done most every job at the SFD — to earn the respect and inspire fellow firefighters.

"When Steve was in charge, he was really good about helping people out and giving you an idea of what the job was," Sutton said. "He worked every position there and was very knowledgeable. He was a good friend. He came and helped me build a house in Manhattan. Most of the firemen helped others out."

Perhaps Steve's most important — and lasting — first impression occurred during his junior year in high school, when Rosie Reyes first gazed at the man who would become her husband.

With his dominant arm in a cast following a wrestling injury, Steve was shooting baskets left-handed one afternoon at Sunset Elementary School.

"He was like Adonis, wearing this tank top, and was really muscular," she recalled. "It was like the sun opened up and said 'awe, here he is.' I thought 'Oh my gosh.' He waited like a month and called me. He was very shy, and I was very shy, and our conversation was not too many words."

They eventually married in 1978 and built a life that includes two sons, Matthew (Matt) and Weston.

"Steve would do anything for those boys. He could work a 24-hour shift, but if they wanted to go out and play pitch-and-catch, he'd go," Rosie said, "and if Steve's right arm got tired, he'd switch to the left."

From coaching his boys and being an ardent fan, Steve snared stellar reviews as a father.

"He never turned us down," Weston said.

Baseball proved to be a strong bond for the Moody boys and their father.

"It was a way for us to do things together. Dad was always coaching me and my brother. He was a baseball fanatic," Weston said.

When Steve and Rosie left Salina, family influenced them to stay close enough to enjoy their sons' college careers at Fort Hays State University, where both played baseball, and Weston was also on the football team.

"Steve was absolutely the best father any boy could want," Rosie said.

Both agreed.

"It was a pretty good experience. Dad's one of the most caring persons you'll ever meet," Weston said. "He was always nice to people, always opening doors for ladies and helping the elderly."

Steve's offspring followed that lead.

"My dad has dealt with a crazy amount of adversity, and what's so amazing is that he's never let it effect how he treated people," Matt said. "From being born with polio, losing his dad when he was only three years old, being overlooked for his dream job, to being afflicted with Lewy body dementia. Most people would become bitter, and he never has."

Steve set a high bar for his sons.

"When it came to my brother and I, there's nothing he didn't do for us. I've always thought that the fact that he never knew his own dad, probably led him to take advantage of all the time he had with us. If we needed him, he was there," Matt said. "If I end up half the dad to my kids as he was to my brother and I, I will be happy. I know most kids think of their dads like Superman, but in our case, he is a very real hero.

We don't even really know how many lives he saved because he did it without expecting any recognition."

The Moody clan today includes five grandkids. Steve and Rosie have kept up with their sons' march through manhood, prowess in business and education (respectively), marriage and parenthood.

Matt, 42, is a co-founder and co-owner of the Salina 311 newspaper and other ventures. Weston, 38, is head football and baseball coach of the Wamego High School Red Raiders.

Steve and Rosie have returned to Salina, and enjoy being within a 72-minute drive to their growing family — Matt and wife Erin, their son Macoy, and daughters Vienna and Lennyn; and Weston and wife Kiley, their daughter Amaia and son Grayson.

Memories are still clear to a couple of Steve's classmates since turning their tassels together at Salina Central High School:

- "Steve is one of the most decent and kind persons I have ever met. He was great to work with when I was a reporter covering accidents and fires, while he was deputy chief at the Salina Fire Department," said Randy Picking, a talk show host at KINA radio in Salina, also a recent inductee into the Kansas Association of Broadcasting Hall of Fame.
- He included a story about Steve's nonchalant reaction to an example of his heroism.
- "Someone shared that Steve was out to dinner with Rosie when another patron began choking. Steve performed the Heimlich maneuver, cleared the man's airway, and then sat back down to finish his meal," Picking said. "He really cares about everyone, and I'm truly lucky to have had the privilege of knowing Steve Moody! Thank-you Chief!"
- Steve was always good to work with when I was a photographer for the Salina Journal. Always helpful," said Tom Dorsey. "The pictures in my mind are the same from when he was a high school classmate and when he was with the Salina Fire Department. He is always smiling."

It was an honor to provide these words. May they whet your appetite to delve into Steve's book and learn more about a great man, loving couple and high-achieving family with much to offer our Kansas community and world.

INTRODUCTION

My name is Steve Moody. I'm 66 years old and I worked for 37 years as a medic and a fire chief with four different departments. During my time worked, I wrote in a journal the experiences that I encountered, both emergency and nonemergency.

Likewise, I wrote about my thoughts on movies, songs, and leadership lessons. I was also an avid reader – reading up to five books a week at one time. I wrote most of the stories during my time as a chief officer to help celebrate annually the accomplishments we made.

The book is broken down into six chapters. Each of the chapters shows stories about times happening during my time in that chapter. Although some of the stories are generic and could've been placed in any of the chapters.

Responding to all of what an emergency responder responds to can take its 'toll one's mind. I believe writing about them and reading about them can help some. And for those readers that are not emergency responders it might help you understand what our heroes encounter.

I hope you enjoy "The Story of my Life."

CHAPTER 1
GROWING UP

POOR FARMER LESSONS

He was a tall lanky farmer. He had fifteen children. He was my grandfather.

A farmer raising fifteen children on land he didn't own was a formula for poverty, but it was also a formula for lessons.

Let me start by describing the farm operation.

Wheat was his "cash crop" so to speak. But he couldn't get by on just raising wheat, especially a farmer with loads of children.

This was back in the good old days when you did it all.

The other parts of the farm operation were primarily focused on feeding all the mouths.

There was a small herd of Holstein cows for milk. Then there was a pig operation for ham and bacon. And a chicken operation that supplied the eggs to go with the bacon. The cows were fifty yards to the west of the home, the chickens twenty yards to the east, and the pigs a bit further away – two hundred yards north.

Equidistant between the house and the pigs was the outhouse.

The shared family car mirrored the compact farm operation – a Honda Rabbit hatchback. On the weekly trip to church, Grandpa would squeeze into the Rabbit with his six-foot two-inch frame, his knees sandwiched between two sun leather arms. It was quite a sight.

The family home's exterior was dull white stucco with bright red trim. Water was accessed by a hand pump out on the back porch. There was one bedroom downstairs for Grandpa and Grandma and two bedrooms upstairs – one for the boys and one for the girls.

Can you see the lessons?

Work ethics were a powerful one. Grandpa didn't talk all that much. He didn't have to. He would work from sunup to sundown. And I never once heard him complain about his plight – never.

Put others before yourself. You can't raise fifteen children on microscopic funds without putting others ahead of yourself.

Frugality is another one. Grandpa and Grandma never had fancy possessions. I doubt there were ever any extra funds. Yet, frugality allowed Grandma to cover their household expenses and still have the dollars to buy a tiny Christmas gift for every single grandchild. And there were a LOT of grandchildren.

Wealth isn't required. Happiness doesn't require running water, a flushing toilet, or a fancy car.

GRANDMA MOODY

My grandmother was a young, divorced mother of three during one of the most difficult times for a mother in America – the depression years. One would think that such a tough life would've left her bitter, but it didn't. She was the same jovial self even later in life when she was stricken with full-scale rheumatoid arthritis.

So, the other day, while going through some old papers, I came across a short story Grandma had given me. And it brought sense to her happiness. The story was called, "There's a Difference."

The story is about two flowers. The time is spring when everything is in full bloom. A young countess comes down the roadway in her

carriage and sees a beautiful apple tree's blossoms. Amazed at the beauty, she breaks off a bough and takes it to her castle where it's placed near a window in a container with other beautiful flowers. The result was the bough became very pleased with itself, not unlike what a human being would do.

People came to the castle to see the flowers and they talked.

Listening, the apple blossom realized the difference between the people. And being near the window the apple blossom was able to look out and see other plants and flowers. It realized there was a difference there too.

One plant was looked down upon. It was a poorly despised weed that was everywhere, and it had a horrible name – the "Devil's Milk Pail". The apple blossom pitied the flower that was so common and carried such an ugly name.

But there was somebody else who saw no difference. His name was sunbeam. And it was said that he kissed the apple blossom, but also kissed the dandelion. And all the sunbeam's brothers kissed them, the poor flowers as well as the rich ones. The sunbeam then tried to convince the apple blossom of the dandelion's beauty.

At first the apple blossom refused to believe the sunbeam. And then a group of children showed their love of the plain dandelion. Then an old woman showed how valuable the dandelion could be. But ultimately the convincing act was when the countess chose to paint the dandelion beside the apple blossom.

Unfortunately, most people in the world think like the apple blossom – they look down on the dandelions. But there are also some who look down on the apple blossoms. For years I was in that group. It took years of maturing for me to finally think like the sun beam. My Grandmother tried to tell me years before by sharing the story "There's a Difference."

MOM

Mom was born on a small farm just east of Salina. She was the first daughter of 15 children. Old pictures often show my mom holding one of her siblings. She simply had to help care for the many babies that came. A mother's role is what she was dealt.

Yet, I never heard my mom speak poorly about her upbringing. Nor did she complain about being a young mother to brother Mike and me.

She provided us with everything we needed. I know she had to have shortened herself to do that. No bitterness.

We were poor but we were happy. Nowadays, there are many folks who have complaint after complaint about their upbringing. I have none. Only appreciation.

Thanks mom.

A CHILD IS BORN

July 12, 1957. I'm told Salina was going through a sweltering heat wave. Today it was 112 degrees. It was also the first day of my life.

The doctor told my father that he couldn't take me home until they got an air conditioner for the home. There was no money to buy one, so he charged one at Otascos.

Women rarely worked outside the home in the 1950's. Living only on my father's income was difficult.

My older brother Mike and I had only a few toys. Everyone has that special toy that stands out well above the rest – your all-time favorite gift. What is it? If the image doesn't come charging out, give it just a moment or two.

For me it arrived on Christmas Day sixty-six years ago. It was a little fellow named Beanie Boy. My brother got the very same gift.

Back in 1961 it was super technology. You pulled on a string and out came a message as the string retracted inwards.

Beanie Boy was so mesmerizing that when my brother and I took our Beanies to the family dinner, all the other kids – and there were many – had to pull the string.

Unfortunately, my brother's Beanie Boy string got pulled a bit too hard or too often. Beanie Boy's string didn't retract. Brother's Beanie Boy became a mute.

I don't know what became of little Beanie Boy. I also don't know why this gift stands out in my mind. He just does.

ROSEBUD

His name was David. He was an engineering aide for Wilson and Co. from Salina, Kansas. The young man had a beautiful wife, two toddler sons, and a decent job. It was a New Year and life was good.

The year 1961 was a time of great fear in America – fear of nuclear war. School children went through drills where they would crouch under their desks with their hands over their heads. And the government was frantically building missile silos at various locations across the country.

One of the missile silo locations under construction was southwest of a small Central Kansas town named Concordia. This silo was in the range of one hundred feet deep. The fear driving the construction of the silos also drove the speed at which construction was conducted. Fast-paced construction with people working over the top of people wasn't a formula for safety.

It was the morning of January 6th. David was working about forty-five feet above the silo floor when an improperly secured two-hundred pound of steel fell from thirty feet above. David was killed instantly when the steel struck him in the head.

David was 25 years old. He was also my father.

This experience taught me from an early age how life could come to an end in the blink of an eye. Three and a half decades of emergency service has given me many reminders. I believe the lesson can be summed up with one word – Rosebud.

You'll have to watch the number one movie of all time, Citizen Kane, to fully understand the meaning of the word. Some of you already have.

The story is about a boy that inherits a fortune. When they come to rescue him from poverty, he's snow sledding. There's a name written on the top of his sled. The message of the story is to never lose focus on what is truly important to you in life.

The name on the top of his sled? *Rosebud*

BROTHER MIKE

I must've been around four years old, since that's about as far back as one can recall a memorable event. And this was the Jim Dandy of memorable events.

The sky was clear blue. A bright sunny spring day – a perfect setting for a family picnic. The flowers at Oakdale Park had burst into full bloom in response to recent heavy rains. That same rain had filled the Smoky Hill Riverbank to bank with fast flowing muddy water.

Parents back in this time didn't entertain-play as much with their children. Children played with children.

So, my older brother and I wandered over to play on the playground equipment. After a short time, we tired of that and decided to explore the nearby river area.

Once at the river's edge we noticed a rather large dead fish floating on top of the water.

I decided to see if I could snare the big beast with a stick. As I neared the shore's skirt the oddest thing happened – the fish disappeared. Unbeknownst to me the rapid waters had washed out a cavity under the edge of the bank.

So, I got down on my hands and knees and leaned out. A little further – a little further – and then it happened.

Face first I plunged into the murky waters. My head was under the water for just a short time, but I can still remember that moment. The swirling brown particles. My eyesight is limited to inches.

Somehow my catapult was such that once righted I was facing and still within reach of shore. My arms revolved around like a Ferris Wheel trying to grab something on the shore. But the recent rain had turned the shore into a virtual oil slick.

All hope seemed lost. And, then it happened.

It was a hand that locked into mine – my brother's hand. A brother who put his own life in danger. Mike reached out to me without regard for his own safety and kept me from being a victim of the Smoky Hill River.

My career in emergency service has spanned thirty-seven years. But, if not for my brother – I would have never been a part of saving any lives as an emergency provider.

The famous Christmas movie named "It's a Wonderful Life" is about a man named George Bailey who does what my brother did – saves his brother from drowning. The movie has a moment when an angel named Clarence asks George, *"Strange, isn't it? Each man's life touches so many other lives. When he isn't around, he leaves an awful hole, doesn't he?"*

A few years ago, I was visiting my brother who lives in Texas. We were enjoying a day at the San Marcos River floating down the rapids on inner tubes. After going through the rapids and drifting downstream, I came to a stop midstream.

Looking back up the river I noticed a mother and small boy hitting the rapids. They fell out of their inner tube and submerged. The boy, still submerged, floated directly at me. When he reached me, I simply reached out and grabbed his arm.

If not for my brother…

UNDERSTANDING PEOPLE

Three decades from now in my story, I would have a going away video that showed a picture of me many, many years ago – as a lean muscular high school wrestler pinning an opponent with a less than kind hold.

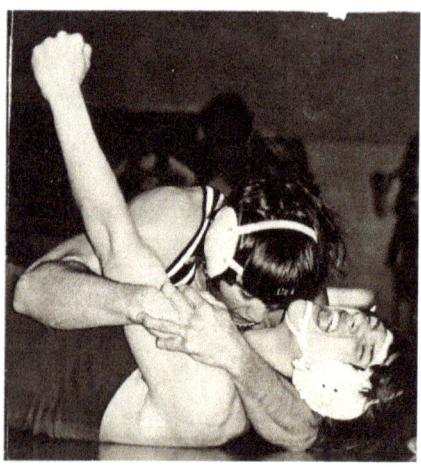

Battalion Chief Ray Hoppe came up to me after the ceremony. He said, "Chief, you were a wrestler. That explains a lot."

The Battalion Chief was correct. Each of our experiences in life has some effect on us, some more than others. One that ranks high is illness. Mine was polio.

Nobody wants to get infected with a disease like polio. But, if you are going to get it, there is a "best time" – and that is when you are the absolute youngest. That was when it came to me.

I was just beginning to walk when my mother noticed my face seemed swollen on the left side. Maybe there was a swollen tooth?

But this was no tooth problem. And the problem wasn't with the left side, it was with the right side – the whole right side of my body. Polio was the problem.

In its course the disease left me with a misshaped body, smaller in all regards on the right side. But the effects weren't just physical, they were also mental – good and bad.

Let us examine the good ones. We will call them lessons.

Empathy was one lesson. Polio left me with a strong sense of empathy for the less fortunate. My sense of empathy became so pronounced that it got me in trouble at times. Folks didn't understand why I responded so vehemently to attacks on the less fortunate.

Polio also taught me the lesson of "triumph over adversity". Who would've thought a young man with size 13 left shoe and a size 10 right shoe, along with an inch and a half shorter leg on the right could ever be a firefighter?

But the most important polio lesson of all was "appreciation". You really get a strong sense of appreciation when you have a disease that has a high likelihood of crippling you but doesn't.

There are so many things that factor into why a person is like they are. Bottom line? Understanding people is complicated.

THE GYM TEACHER

I've already told you that my father died when I was three years old. He was a surveyor and was working in the bottom of a missile silo when a two-hundred-pound piece of steel accidentally dropped from the top of the silo. The piece of steel struck him in the head and killed him instantly.

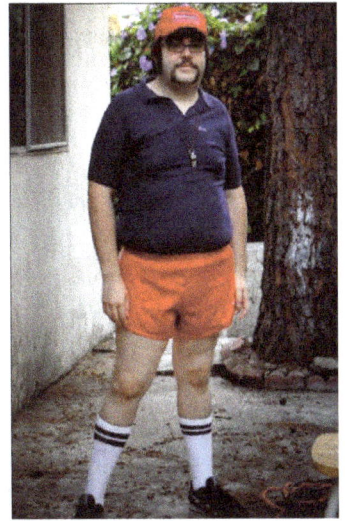

I know this from reading the obituary that my grandmother gave me after I reached adulthood. Unfortunately, I have no memory of him.

Back in that time you didn't collect a big check – or any check – after your spouse died on the job. My mother did a great job raising me and my brothers. We had everything we needed. But we did live in one of the poorer parts of town. Not that it mattered. I didn't even realize that my family was poor – until I went to middle school.

My gym teacher in middle school was a short, paunchy fellow who thought he was God's gift to women. The pompous fool was constantly trying to swoon at the girl's gym teacher. This didn't bother me. What bothered me was how he started each class period.

At the beginning of class, we were instructed to sit down on the basketball court to witness the daily competition. The Gym Teacher and one of the wealthy kids would shoot free throws until one missed. This would go on for quite some time because they were both quite good shots. The experience instilled in me a dislike of the wealthy.

I'm ashamed to say that this feeling lived on in me for many years. It even manifested itself through my two sons.

I coached my sons in competitive little league baseball. Our team was comprised of players from average to lower income level families. I know part of my drive for success for the team was fueled by my long-ago experience with The Gym Teacher.

When an opposing team would roll into the baseball parking lot in a custom bus and step out with their embroidered uniforms and custom ball bags – my energy level would surge. On most occasions we came out victorious. Unfortunately, it didn't seem to ease the pain.

That all changed when a career step took me into administration. I was soon interacting with many people who were in the upper wealth category. I realized that it wasn't the rich kid that was the problem back in middle school, it was the Gym Teacher.

As a Leader you have many core responsibilities. No responsibility is greater than that of "Fairness." Whether it be a class of middle school kids or a team of workers, nobody likes to be forced to see an individual receive preferential treatment.

Everyone serves in a leadership position at times during their life. Occasionally, ask yourself, "Does anyone see me as – The Gym Teacher?"

THE POWER OF A SIMPLE ACT

I don't recall the exact day that it took place. It was such a simple act that it didn't seem to have any great significance. I was mowing my lawn on the side that blended into my neighbor's. Their usually well-manicured lawn was unusually tall. But I didn't think much about it because I heard the gentleman of the house had recently had some type of surgery. And I was also aware the couple was retired and had no children.

So, without much thought, I decided it wouldn't take much longer to knock out their lawn too. I hadn't finished a couple passes when the lady of the house appeared on the front porch. I stopped my mower, not knowing what to expect. Was she happy with what I was doing, or was she going to throw me off her property?

As I approached the front porch, I noticed she was noticeably upset. As the tears rolled down her face she thanked me, or at least that's what it sounded like through the sobs.

I thought it was unusual for her to be so appreciative of such a simple act. And I told her that in a kind sort of way. What I didn't know while standing on the lawn that day was the power of that simple act.

Her name was Jeanne. Husband Smoke had indeed had a recent surgery. It was knee replacement surgery. Smoke made it through the surgery and back to his room without a hitch. But that night he suffered a massive stroke from a blood clot that left the surgery site and traveled to his brain. He never recovered and died after a long stint of convalescence.

Jeanne and Smoke not only had no children, but they also had no relatives – other than a sister and a couple of nieces a thousand miles away on the east coast. And so, it evolved.

The lawn mowing continued. Another plate was placed on the table during the holidays. And a very special relationship developed.

What my family and I discovered was one of the most unique and wonderful people we'd ever met. Our relationship lasted a lifetime. My wife and I had a second mother, and my children had a third grandmother. And Jeanne had us.

And to think it all started with a simple act.

THE KING'S SPEECH

I was watching an award-winning movie called "The King's Speech" a couple days ago. It's a movie about Britain's King George VI and a problem he had. The King had a serious speech stammer.

Fortunately, the King was able to overcome the affliction with the help of an Australian speech therapist named Lionel Logue. Through Lionel's help, instead of being a laughingstock to the public, the King was able to give an epic speech declaring war against Germany.

GROWING UP

The movie has several messages. To me the strongest message is how one of the most famous people in history owed his greatness to a support person. So, who are those in your shadow?

Like most people, I've had many who've been in my shadow. But I will tell you about just one, the most important one. I have known this

person for many, many – many years.

We first met on a grade school playground in 1970. As a girl of fourteen she didn't know then what a tremendous role she would play in my life. Her name is Rosalia, but most know her as Rosie – or the Chief's wife.

Rosie has always worked behind the scenes and has always been supportive of whatever was needed to bolster my career. Yet, she's never had a title, never had a badge, and she's never gotten any recognition other than that given by me. That this lack of recognition is okay with her is what makes what she does, and has done, even more special.

In the King's speech to his people, he talks of the "...*mere primitive doctrine that might is right.*" Those in the limelight are often in the "might." But you must not use you might un-rightly, nor should you fail to recognize those in your shadow – those who were instrumental in your success.

Have you recognized those people who've played an instrumental part in your life?

Another statement in King VI's famous speech says, "For the sake of all that we ourselves hold dear, it is unthinkable that we should refuse to meet the challenge." I say let us apply "the challenge" to recognizing those in your shadow.

Do it soon. Tomorrow might be a good day.

THE LITTLE RED BOOK

My grandfather had an eye for the ladies – ladies other than my grandmother. So, after a few years Grandma gave him his walking papers. Unfortunately, Gramps was a virile fellow too. He produced three children before his quick departure – two boys and one girl. The girl's name was Elizabeth. I called her Aunt Lizzie.

Lizzie worked her way through college – a feat made easier from watching her single mother successfully raise three children on a nursing home aide salary. Lizzie learned another lesson from her mother – the lesson of giving small gifts.

Every Christmas as a child I received a little red book from Aunt Lizzie. The stories were short, and the theme was always about adventure. Subsequently, I developed a love of reading that has lasted a lifetime. But, at the time I failed to realize the sacrifice Lizzie was making to buy me that book, or the impact of the gift.

The light finally came on when I was reading a newly purchased book. The name of the book was "The World According to Mister Rogers." It was little. It was red.

I was ashamed that I had never told Lizzie what her gifts meant to me. So, I bought another copy of Mister Rogers and sent it to Lizzie – along with a note. Three days later she called. Lizzie's speech is like a roller coaster – the tone goes up and down with great excitement. She loved her little red book.

Six months later I received another telephone call. This one was different. It was more like a roller coaster stalled at the top of the tracks – idle and tense. Lizzie didn't mince words. She explained that she had been to the doctor because of back pain. The doctor diagnosed late-stage pancreatic cancer.

With the strength of a field general she said, "I have a great team of doctors and I'm going to fight this enemy with all my might. But we need to be realistic too. The doctors have given me 3-6 months and few people beat pancreatic cancer."

Almost six months to the day of her phone call, Lizzie died.

Before her death Lizzie developed a financial education program for high school students. She traveled the United States teaching teachers how to deliver the program. The training and all the materials were provided free of charge.

Lizzie's overall legacy was the impact she had on thousands of high school students. Her legacy with me was "The Little Red Book." Another person who had a reading impact upon me was my 3rd grade teacher - Mrs. Dolan. She had a yearly reading contest. I won the contest my third-grade school year. Forever afterwards I have loved reading.

HANDS ON THE WALL

My youngest son was teaching for a month in the summer at an orphanage in Brazil. While there he took a picture of what he thought was an  empty courtyard. Later – he noticed the hands of a youth hanging onto the top of the stone wall.

The photo made me wonder how many times we miss the "hands on the wall."

Author Bill Bryson's A Short History of Nearly Everything notes that an average human life lasts just 650,000 hours. Can we afford to miss the details in our experiences?

What if we didn't miss those hands?

Maybe it would lead to a long-term friendship. Maybe it would lead to helping somebody. Maybe it would give you a smile. Maybe it would nourish your soul. Or give you a heart-felt tear.

I told my son to let the photo be a reminder to take in every single detail of his experience during his time in Brazil. Be on the look-out for the "Hands on the Wall."

Not bad advice for all of us – including myself.

WAMEGO HIGH SCHOOL SUB-STATE FOOTBALL GAME

The night was a frigid one, but I was well-dressed. Wamego was undefeated and after the night was done, the undefeated season of 12-0 stood strong.

Son Weston had coached Wamego to its best ever football season.

With encouragement from older son Matt, I proceeded to the field to hug Weston for his great accomplishment.

YOU GOTTA LOVE THE MUTTS

Jackie Mo, Jack Sprat, Jacky Poo, and A.J.

He had many names, but his actual name was simply "Jackson." We named him after President Andrew Jackson, always a favorite of mine. He was the runt of the litter – a litter born at a small rural Kansas farm. His brothers and sisters had been sold to a wholesaler in Kansas City, but Jackson was left behind because he had a skin ailment.

Jackson was a gift to my wife for her birthday. Rosie said he was the best gift she ever received. Jackson was not much larger than your hand and was the deepest coal black you could imagine, with eyes that matched. Before we headed home, I brought him to the high school where Rosie worked. It was love at first sight, a love that lasted a lifetime.

As a puppy Jackson had a fetish for the buttons on the top of baseball caps – not the ball cap itself, just the button. With two boys who played competitive baseball, there was plenty of buttons to consume at the Moody house. For some reason the boys didn't have a great desire to wear their caps without the buttons.

GROWING UP

Jackson attended just about every baseball game our boys ever played. All the parents and players looked forward to seeing Jackson. He didn't know a stranger and that may have been why he was never a nervous, yippy dog.

Jackson was a miniature schnauzer, a breed that's the epitome of a perfect firefighter. They are put together in a small, super musculature package. They also seem to have the bravery of your best firefighters. Even in old age, Jackson never met a dog that he feared. A case in point was the day a neighbor walked his four- foot-tall wolf dog past our unfenced back yard.

Jackson was fourteen years old at the time and had lost his hearing. When Jackson saw Cujo, he lopped across the yard without an ounce of fear to check him out. I launched full speed from the deck knowing that any volume of hollering was useless.

Unfortunately, I didn't get there in time. Cujo grabbed Jackson by his back like a chew toy and hoisted him high off the ground. I pried open Cujo's mouth as the owner screamed at him to let go. Fortunately, Jackson had on a Christmas sweater that buffered the assault.

Even though he was a tuff fellow that had no fear, Jackson's real legacy was his calmness that was created by Rosie holding him. She would hold him like a baby in her arms and rub his belly. My how he loved his belly rubbed. But Rosie was the only one who held him like that, for others he would just push up beside you and roll to his back for the belly rub.

Rosie took great responsibility with Jackson, a responsibility level that others should strive to emulate. She always told me that she would never let Jackson get to a point where he would suffer from old age ailments.

Jackson was sixteen years old and had lost his hearing, had serious cataracts, and had lost control of his bladder. I came home from lunch and found Rosie holding Jackson like she always did. Except this day it was different. She had a deep sadness in her face, a sadness I had never seen. She told me it was time.

Later that day we took Jackson to the veterinarian. Before we left, I cut a small tuff off his hair and tied it in a loop. When we got to the treatment room, we each held a paw as the vet gave Jackson the medicine. Rosie kissed his face as he peacefully took his last breath.

We learned a lot from Jackson. We learned unconditional love, fearlessness, calmness, and the ability to show the greatest of happiness with something as insignificant as a popsaroni treat. There have been others that followed, but there was never another Jackson.

"We really miss you Jackson, Thanks for the memories."

SHRINE BOWL HEAD COACH RECOGNITION EVENT

Weston Moody was recognized at the Wamego high school for being chosen as the Head Coach for the East Squad. Family Kiley, Amaia, and Grayson joined in the festive event.

EARLY LEADERSHIP LESSONS

I've loved the game of baseball from an early age. I started coaching at an early age too. I don't know how old I was in this picture. It was when I started coaching my younger brother, Tim.

We practiced on the sandlot diamond at Sunset School. The boys all lived in close walking distance to the school. The picture makes me think of the great baseball show "Sand Lot."

I'm towards the back in a gray jacket and fellow friend/coach Larry

Henoch is on the left side wearing the red jacket. The leadership lessons from baseball started at an early age.

I continued coaching my son's team. My fellow friends Ed Nave and Tim Buyse were two fellow coaches that helped me coach the team until they advanced into upper age Legion players.

Chuck Donmeyer, that was the year between Football at Dodge City and KSU. That job has followed me throughout my adult life, the joy and satisfaction I get out of a building project, renovation or simply just fixing something, I owe that joy to you.

I could go on and on with more stories and the fact is that you, Rosemary and Dave did so much and encouraged me as a kid, it is a debt I'll never be able to repay. I know you are not well and this brings me much sadness but looking back and remembering what a great life I have lived and the contribution that you have made, really fills my heart with joy. Thank you Steve for all the great times and memories, you are one of the good guys and will never be forgotten, certainly not by me or anyone else who has had the pleasure of knowing you.

Sincerely,
Rob

FAST EDDIE

It was the late 1970's and adult slow-pitch softball was just getting popular in Salina. The great thing about slow-pitch – versus fast pitch – is you don't have to be much of an athlete to play the game – sorry slow pitch players, that's the painful truth.

Almost all the slow-pitch teams had sponsors. One team was called "The Peacock" after their sponsor, a bar on North Broadway. The team was a mixture of firefighters and friends of firefighters.

The word "average" is probably a generous description for most of the players on the team. Our shortstop was a friend of the firefighters by the name "Eddie Koelling."

Eddie would buzz around the base paths with short, rapid strides which made him appear to be faster than he was. Nevertheless, we called him "Fast Eddie." He got this nickname not because of his blazing speed, but because of his occupation – Car Salesman.

It was typical of firemen to give out nicknames. And Eddie's nickname was just fun because Eddie was the opposite of somebody who would slicker you.

For some time, here of late, our shortstop "Fast Eddie" had been competing against a bigger opponent than we ever did on the slow-pitch diamond. The opponent's name was "Cancer."

Eddie gave the opponent as good a game as anybody could have. But every game has its' ending and this one ended yesterday.

Someday all of us will see our game come to an end. We can only hope that we play the game as well as "Fast Eddie" – The Peacock Shortstop.

GUARDIAN ANGELS

The place was Guadalajara, Mexico. My son was on an educaJonal visit meandering through the market square. Food is the main item peddled by the merchants, but it's a good spot to see just about anything for sell – even a Chihuahua.

There they were. Four tiny puppies dressed in miniature sombreros. One of them – Felipe – was soon to meet a guardian angel – my son.

The permission for the purchase was secured with a quick call back to Kansas. The two of them boarded an airplane for the trip back to America once Felipe got his clearance from a local vet. Felipe made the ride back in an orange foam basket, sitting quietly on Weston's lap.

Weston was still a college student, so Felipe ended up living with mom and dad. And the love he brought was only matched by the love he received.

So, do you believe in angels?

The Christmas season brings with it many wonderful movies. One is called "The Bishop's Wife." It's a story about an Episcopalian Bishop who prays to God for an angel to help him build a cathedral. And that's what he gets – an angel.

The guardian angel appears as a man named Dudley. Dudley helps the Bishop – not exactly in the way he wished, but in a grander fashion. When his work is done and he leaves earth, Dudley erases the memories of him with all he interacted with.

The premise of the story is that God works his miracles through mysterious ways – ways you might not be aware. The story concludes with a sermon read by the Bishop – one written by Dudley.

Here's that sermon.

Tonight, I want to tell you the story of an empty stocking. Once upon a midnight clear, there was a child's cry, a blazing star hung over a stable, and wise men came with birthday gifts.

We haven't forgotten that night down the centuries. We celebrate it with stars on Christmas trees, with the sound of bells, and with gifts – especially with gifts.

You gave me a book; I will give you a tie. Aunt Martha has always wanted an orange squeezer and Uncle Henry can do with a new pipe. For we forget nobody, adult, or child.

All the stockings are filled, all that is, except one. And we have even forgotten to hang it up – the stocking for the child born in a manger.

It's his birthday we're celebrating. Don't let us ever forget that.

Let us ask ourselves what "He" would wish for most. And then, let each put in his share – loving kindness, warm hearts, and a stretched-out hand of tolerance – all the shining gifts that make peace on earth.

MY BEST FRIEND

Her long dark hair gently flowed in the warm summer Kansas breeze. First straight behind her, then straight ahead wrapping around her beau-

tiful, brown-skinned face. She was riding one of the playground swings.

This was my first encounter with a girl named Rosie Reyes.

We both lived within a block of Sunset Grade School. Rosie was in the sixth grade; I was in the eighth. The number eight turned out to be a special number for us.

Eight years later I walked the little girl

down the long, long center aisle at Sacred Heart Cathedral after saying, "I do."

Forty-five years later the count continues. So, what are the highlights of this voyage?

FUN
Boy, have we had a lot. The great thing about fun is it doesn't have to cost anything. If you are doing something as simple as going for a walk with the one you love – that's fun. There's been trips, events, celebrations, excursions, and walks – thousands and thousands of them.

TEAMWORK
It's a small team of two, but it's a team. Your success as a team means that sometimes one person must give more than the other. My partner was the epitome of giving. Rosie was never called Fire Chief, but when called the Chief's Wife those words carried more meaning than most knew.

CHILDREN
The team can grow. Children aren't required, but they sure add a lot to life. Our two sons brought us a wealth of loving memories one could never place a price tag. Now there are two grandsons, and three granddaughters.

HARDSHIP
You must work together with all your inner strength to overcome hardships. That digging deep within to overcome is what can build togetherness in every respect of the word. When two people with no money get married and afterwards take lifetime governmental jobs – that's a recipe for togetherness.

LOVE
The word is abused, but in its truest sense it's a great summation. It includes fun, it includes teamwork, it includes children, and it includes hardship. I believe it also means Best Friends.

Forty-five years plus the count continues. And it will until one of our hearts beats no longer.

MY BEST FRIEND – A GIRL NAMED ROSIE.

CHAPTER 2
MY CAREER IN SALINA

THE BEGINNING

The beginning was October of 1978. I had just turned 21 years old, had 3 months of marriage under my belt, and knew little about being a firefighter. My neighbor was Lavern Brockway who was the Salina Interim Fire Chief and that's what sparked my interest. I was working construction building houses and winter was coming soon. And with that would be weather-related layoffs. I needed a stable job.

So, if selected, I would take a pay cut from my construction job and figure I would make it up working a secondary construction job like almost all the other firefighters did. All I needed to do was climb the aerial truck fully extended and simple doctor's exam.

But more about what I needed to do to become a Salina firefighter after telling you the story about one of two Salina firefighters who have died in the line of duty. I call it the "Mitchel Questionnaire" to give a lesson on how to keep one safer when responding to an emergency.

THE MITCHEL QUESTIONNAIRE

The big gong slammed the sides of the brass bell as it rocked back and forth in its cradle. The message "wasn't" that it was lunch time. This was a fire message and the firefighters heard it.

Two of the responders were Fred Brodbeck and Raymond Miller – SFD fire chief and driver. Their means of travel was a Mitchell car with a custom rear bed that carried firefighting equipment. This was a custom addition designed by the chief.

They raced down Ohio Street and just as they were approaching the Iron Street Bridge a horse and buggy pulled onto the street. Miller swerved but the car caught the rear of the buggy and launched the car down the banks of the Smoky Hill River.

Brodbeck was seriously injured in the accident and was taken to the hospital. But this was well before we knew how to treat infection. Gangrene set in and the chief died five days later at the age of 39.

Brodbeck came to Salina, Kansas from Chicago. The local press chronicled the innovative things he implemented. Many of them were successful, but unfortunately one was the Mitchell modification.

Those in wild land firefighting must be master innovators too. Standard trucks are converted into fire trucks. Military trucks are converted into fire trucks. All-terrain vehicles are converted into fire trucks.

Most of our changes are good, but are there possibly some Mitchell modifications? Before you make modifications to a truck ask yourself some questions.

Have you exceeded the vehicle's weight capacity? Turning ability could be adversely affected. Braking could be adversely affected. Rollover potential could be heightened.

Are undercarriage components heat resistant? Plastic brake lines could melt from heat. Fuel lines could do the same. This could happen at the most inopportune time, possibly endangering the lives of firefighters.

Have you designed rear-riding locations properly? Handrails must be present and must be adequate. Some type of belting system needs to be present. Sharp cornered impact points should be eliminated or covered.

Are you changing a key operational component? You should not change the size of a truck's tires without getting a stamp of approval from the manufacturer. Too small tires might cause a heat build-up on brake pads.

Let a picture of the Brodbeck accident be your visual reminder. Prepare a list of safety questions before making any truck modifications. A good name for it might be The Mitchell Questionnaire.

ONE HUNDRED FOOT CHALLENGE

She was parked on the west side of the hose tower. The rays of the sun were shining down through the open cab upon the black leather seats. The truck was stabilized by an arm on both sides with giant threads which appeared to be adjustable if you had a giant wrench.

The ladder was extended upwards almost to the edge of the sun. I was told the driver aimed for the sun when he extended her, but in her old age she had developed a slight arch when extended the full one hundred foot. So, the ladder tip ended up just to the left side of the sun.

Next to the base of the ladder on both sides were two red tubes that looked like grenade launchers. These were the hydraulic cylinders that raised and lowered the ladder.

If I wanted to be a firefighter, my task would be simple. I needed to climb to the top, touch the tip, then climb down. All in less than ten minutes.

But there's something strange about climbing a gigantic ladder – especially a crooked one – that's sticking straight up into the air. And stranger yet, it's not leaning against a supportive structure – like a building.

All kinds of thoughts go through your brain. What if one of those tiny support arms fails? What if one of the hydraulic cylinders holding up the ladder sprouts a leak? Thoughts turn to fear.

The palms began to perspire. The heartbeat increased – both in rate and intensity. And I got a big lump in my throat. Did I really want to be a firefighter?

Yes, was the answer. But it wasn't a deep manly yes – it was more like a grade schoolgirl yes.

So, I climbed up to the turntable. As I stood at the base the very top wasn't quite visible. I was just about to change my mind when the timekeeper asked, "Are you ready?" Right before I gave the "thumbs up", I told myself the death would at least be instant.

The first fifty feet went fast. A handrail on both sides gave me a sense of security. This wasn't too bad after all. But the ladder started to narrow. And then the side rail was no longer.

The sun was getting closer as the ladder shimmied down to what seemed to be a size that fit my preboarding childlike voice. I had reached the curve point. And it made me feel like there was a super magnet pulling me towards the left.

It was at that point the timekeeper shouted, "Five-minute mark!" I refused to look down. Up, up, up another sixteen feet. The red painted tip was now in reach. I stretched my arm until I feared it would disconnect from the socket. Slowly my fingers encircled the rung.

Looking down at the pea-sized timekeeper he appeared to wave his hand. That was enough acknowledgement for me.

The speed of the trip up the ladder was like a turtle stampeding through peanut butter. The one down the ladder was liken a rabbit being chased by a beagle. Within what seemed like seconds I was standing next to the timekeeper.

All that remained was to ensure he saw me reach the top. And he did.

We all go through challenges in life. In many ways facing and overcoming those challenges is what molds us.

My career as a firefighter began with a "One Hundred Foot Challenge."

REMEMBERING SALINA FIRE CHIEF LAVERNE BROCKWAY

By Steve Moody and Willis Sutton

Laverne Brockway, a distinguished member of the Salina Fire Department from 1957 to 1982, passed away this past Sunday.

His career was marked by perseverance and leadership, culminating in his retirement as the Acting Fire Chief.

During his tenure, Brockway experienced significant changes in operational schedules. Initially, his duties were structured around 24-hour shifts, alternating with 24 hours off. In the late 1960s, this shifted to a 24-on, 48-off rotation, accommodating summer vacations through a cooperative arrangement among shifts.

Brockway's commitment extended beyond his scheduled hours, as he remained on call through a Plectron Radio at home. His career trajectory saw him advance to the role of Fire Inspector in 1967 and ultimately to Fire Chief in 1978.

His tenure was rich with anecdotes and lessons.
- Brockway often recounted the early days of the department, highlighting the challenges of building fire trucks with only hand tools and demonstrating life-saving techniques like using fire extinguishers and jumping into rescue nets during Fire Prevention Week. (The equipment of the era was sparse, with only one air-pack per truck, reserved for victim rescue).
- One notable memory involved the "mask marvel", Chief Travis, during the JC Penny's Fire. Brockway vividly remembered how the crew he was on had been working to break the rear door in for access to the fire. After some time had passed, Chief Travis said "Give me that damn axe" and with two hits the door was down.
- Brockway fondly recalled initiating newcomers like Jim Weese into the demanding and smoky conditions of firefighting. One such instance was at the Allied Truck Fire, where Brockway, ever the embodiment of cool under pressure, casually greeted his crew amidst intense smoke while enjoying a cigar and a "How you boys doing?"

Chief Brockway's service was characterized by an unwavering dedication to public safety. Working alongside a team of equally committed individuals, he exemplified the qualities of a firefighter: bravery, heroism, and camaraderie. These virtues were not just a part of the job but were amplified in an era that cherished them even more.

Reflecting on Chief Brockway's legacy, it is evident that he was more than just a firefighter; he was a hero and a role model. His impact and the deep sense of unity he fostered within the department have left an indelible mark on those who knew him, securing him a cherished place in their memories. Chief Brockway was also the Chief that hired Will Sutton, I and many others.

SPARKLES

I passed the aerial climb and the doctor's exam and was officially a Salina firefighter. My first day as a firefighter was spent at the airport fire station. The station was a lime green leftover from the Schilling Military Airbase. A vast building that even had a flight tower.

The station officer was a slightly–built fellow who was a master ping- pong player; the driver a heavy-set fellow with the moves of an NBA point guard – a few of our after-hour activities during our 24-hour tour of duty. The last crew member was a bit shorter than the other two

– and had four legs. Her name was Sparky.

Sparky was short by Dalmatian standards. The firefighters had a love or hate relationship with Sparky. Mine was love. So, it was a sad day for me when several years later Sparky was hit and killed by a motorist. Sparky made her mark on many firefighters. After her death, I vowed that one day I would have a Dalmatian.

Dalmatians were a tough breed to find back in the 1980's – and expensive. Four hundred dollars was just a bit pricey for my minimum wage salary. Then, after several years of searching, I found an ad that listed Dalmatian puppies for sale. As had been my habit with choosing dogs, I opted for the smallest of the litter and named her Sparkles.

Dalmatians have the energy of two or three dogs – they're always on alert and they never seem to relax. Sparkles showed her energy and fun-loving attitude at a young age. My wife bought an expensive bed comforter and before using it she washed it and placed it on the clothesline to dry. The comforter would warm us for years to come – or would it?

Hours after hanging the comforter, a neighbor knocked on our door to inform us there was something terribly wrong. She said it looked like a snowstorm had hit our backyard – and it was July. Sparkles had turned our new comforter into a million and one cotton balls.

Emergency services tend to attract those whose motor runs at a fast speed. Some of these folks will be even higher paced than others. These would be your Sparkles employees. They might be branded as "suck-ups" because they are always doing more than others.

Sparkles energy and desire to please made her a perfect fit for public education. I taught her to "Stop, Drop & Roll" and the kids loved her. She was equally fit for my two young sons. Whatever our family did in the backyard, Sparkles was there to help us. When we dug a water-well, she was right there watching us every step of the way, helping by digging in the sand.

She was fourteen when the medical problems started. First, a large tumor appeared on the right side of her chest. It didn't seem to hurt her, but it did bother her when she walked very far. Half-way through a moderate walk she would start limping. Sometimes, I would have to carry her to make it around the block.

Then, she started having trouble with her bladder leaking. I called the veterinarian hoping that he would encourage me to make the choice of putting her down. He didn't. He suggested putting her on medication. It didn't help.

She struggled through the fall season, but as we headed into the winter it looked like she was going to notch her 16th birthday. Then it happened.

The night was the coldest I could remember. A late-night house fire blocks away from my own home resulted in the death of an elderly man. I got back home after the house fire at around midnight and went to bed. For some reason my wife woke up at 4am to find Sparkles lying on her side on the concrete patio. She cried for me to come quickly.

I launched from bed faster than I ever had in my firefighter career. I scooped up Sparkles in my arms and brought her into the house. My sons had awakened too. I held her tight to my own body trying to quickly warm her. Her eyes were open but glazed over. As I tried my best to warm her, Sparkles took her last breath. The whole family cried.

The Sparkles are your top performers, the ones that leave their mark on the world. When they leave the organization, you wonder if their departure will cause a total collapse. It won't.

To Sparkles and those like her, "Thanks for the memories."

SFD HISTORY BOOK

In 1993 me and paramedic Greg Brockway produced a book on the history of the SFD. We did research at the Salina Public Library plus interviews with retirees.

I wrote the book with assistance from English school teacher Bev Davis. Greg did the photography work.

The book was produced by Jostin's book production company.

It's the only known book of history on the SFD.

GREAT BATTALION CHIEF

As a Deputy Chief it was my responsibility to give yearly evaluations to Battalion Chiefs. The name of one was Jim Weese. It was a pleasure to put his evaluation together.

Jim did his job as Battalion Chief masterfully. He understood leadership and could give classes on it. He had his shift working as a team like no other. One could say, "Their hearts were beating as one."

Jim would do special things with his men that helped them bond. He would take on special projects without a glimmer of resistance. The amazing thing about Jim's performance was what he did on his days off. Jim ran a successful construction business. Jim could've easily been a fire chief if he had wanted.

Now, to be fair, Jim's construction partnership was with fellow SFD member Lieutenant Chuck Donmyer. Chuck helped him make doing both jobs possible.

That's the wonderful thing about the fire service. One can run a business on their days off. I could name off many SFD firefighters who ran highly successful off-duty businesses.

But none that did it as a Battalion Chief.

I was a lucky man to have Jim as one of my Battalion Chiefs.

THUMPERS TO GOOGLE GLASSES

Somebody famous once said, "There are three signs of old age. Loss of memory...I forget the other two.

After having yet ANOTHER birthday – it seems like those damn things come every year – it's becoming ever clearer that I'm getting rather ancient.

This was highlighted this past week when I attended advanced pediatric life support training at Hutchinson Hospital. All but one of my fellow students were young enough to be

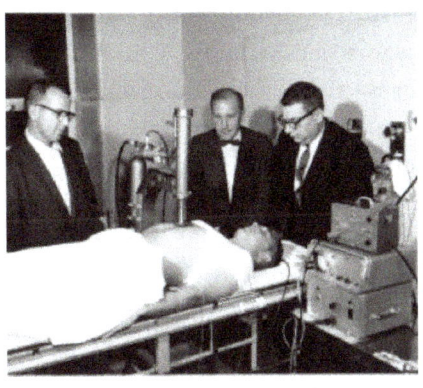

my children. The one other senior student was not only my age – he was also named "Steven."

Every time Steven thought of an "old way of doing things" he quizzically turned to me and asked, "Do you remember that?" Thumpers, MAST Trousers, Sodium Bicarb formulas, and on, and on. Yes, yes, yes was always my answer.

Old medical workers might seem a bit confused at times, but you'd be confused too if you had learned multiple ways of doing things – often conflicting with what was previously taught. I might have maxed out my hard drive simply with the 64 versions of how to do CPR.

If a person wanted to make a lot of money – and help us senior folks – they would invent a delete device that selectively withdraws antiquated data from your brain.

But somebody not so famous – me – says, "If you want to stay in the game, then you have to adapt to change." So, I learned from the instructors in the PALS class and passed the examination.

And speaking of new things. My oldest son recently made a trip to San Francisco to pick up a new piece of technology. It's called "Google Glasses." He was one of a select group that was chosen to be the initial recipients of this space age equipment.

I don't know exactly how they work, but he has promised to bring them out to Stafford County. So, let me know if you want a demonstration.

DUMMY HEADING

President Roosevelt - "It is not the critic who counts; not the man who points out how the strong man stumbles, or where the doer of deeds could have done them better. The credit belongs to the man who is actually in the arena, whose face is marred by dust and sweat and blood; who strives valiantly; who errs, who comes short again and again, because there is no effort without error and shortcoming; but who does actually strive to do the deeds; who knows great enthusiasms, the great devotions; who spends himself in a worthy cause; who at the best knows in the end the triumph of high achievement, and who at the worst, if he fails, at least fails while daring greatly,
Crystal VanCoevern, LMSW

HALLOWEEN FIRE SAFETY HOUSE

The Halloween Fire Safey House was a public education event that had music, actors in costume, and rooms. There were 5 separate rooms that small groups of 3 to 5 children were escorted through by costumed

guides. The event was the brainchild of public educator Deb Weaver and her husband Bill.

The event was put on 3 nights with one of the nights being Halloween. Over 3,000 people went through the fire education show. It was a huge success.

WHO'S DIRECTING YOUR TRAFFIC?

It was just before noon at one of the busiest intersections in town. An impressive accident had just occurred when a silver mini-van t-boned a red truck – tipping it onto its side. Both van and truck were loaded with occupants, so more ambulances would be needed to transport all the non- critical patients.

This wasn't an incident that called for an administrative officer, but the accident was in alignment with my trip back to the office. So, I stopped to observe, but shooting a video of what I was watching – for the responders to later watch – seemed like a good idea too.

Another ambulance was needed for patient transport, but it seemed like there was more than an ample number of emergency personnel on scene. Heck, there were even several civilian helpers on scene.

I immediately spied on one of the civilians who had pitched in to help. He was directing traffic. Then another jumped in. Then another jumped in. Three civilian traffic directors with – no vests and no identification.

This incident took place years ago. Nobody got hurt and it isn't my intention to show this video to embarrass anyone. The responders are some of the bests I have worked with in my thirty-four-year career.

I'm showing the video to remind my current department members, and any others who might watch it, that even the "best responders" can oversee the mundane, but important roles during an emergency.

Who's directing your emergency traffic?

MOST DANGEROUS FIRES

It was a clear, sunny midday spring afternoon. Fellow friend/firefighter Rick and I were assigned to the tailboard of Rescue 1. We were at fire station 2 because Engine 2 needed to be at fire station 1.

The alarm was sounded, "We have a report of a fire in a basement Highland Cr." This was located around 10 blocks away.

We were upstairs, so we quickly slid on the pole down to the apparatus floor, donned our fire gear, and jumped on the tailboard.

The house was just 10 blocks away and we could see smoke on the horizon. On arrival we were met in the front yard by the homeowner, and he said, "The fire is in the basement." And he directed us to a door on the side of the home. The door was open, and smoke was billowing out.

Rick and I returned to Rescue 1 where we donned our air packs, grabbed a hose line, and returned and entered through the open door.

Down the basement steps we made our way to the very back reach of the basement. It was there, in the back room, that we found a small fire. I was holding the fire hose, and I opened the nozzle, quickly extinguishing the fire.

Other responding crews had made it to the scene because Rick and I could hear them in the outer basement. One of the firefighters, Gene, made it back to the room where we were – just on the other side of the room.

The smoke had started to dissipate when Rick nudged me and pointed to the floor. It was a weight scale. Then it happened.

It was a loud whooshing noise. We looked out through the room's doorway and instantaneously a monstrous fireball consumed the outer room. And within seconds it immediately blew into our room, totally engulfing it too.

Gene panicked which caused him to fall flat on his back where he wallowed like a capsized turtle. I opened the nozzle and directed it straight at Gene.

Seconds later Rick made a mad dash over to help Gene to his feet. I was directing the nozzle at both. Once Rick had Gene standing, they both returned to a position behind me where they had the safety of the nozzle.

In the meantime, Rick jumped up on a box that was beneath a small window. But it was clearly too small. Rick remembered what one of his officers once told him, "Turn your nozzle to a fog stream if you get trapped in a basement." So, he reached around me and turned the nozzle to fog.

Less than two minutes later we had the fire extinguished. Rick later said that right before the fire ball, he was going to take his gloves and air pack off. Luckily, none of us did.

We all made it back to the outside where we were treated for primary and secondary burns.

Once all the smoke was ventilated, we discovered a large-scale drug operation. Marijuana was being processed in a half-dozen 55-gallon barrels.

Gene and I were taken to the hospital with first and secondary burns. Rick stayed on scene.

A chemist from Kansas Wesleyan University was brought to the scene to help identify the hazardous materials. The chemist told Rick that had the glass bottles broken in the box he had been standing on, there would have been an explosion that would have certainly killed all three of us.

Basement fires – one of firefighters' most dangerous.

Responding to a "close call" brings a firefighter closeness, a bond. Rick & Gene will forever be good friends.

REMEMBERING PONCHO

Twenty years ago, the holidays were in full swing. Three-year-old Poncho's mother Twilia had just acquired a job at a local nursing home. She dropped Poncho and his older brother Rogue off at the babysitter.

Her name was Charity. Charity's four-year-old daughter Monique and the boys were playing upstairs later that morning when it happened.

The investigation revealed that the three children started the fire in a closet with a lighter. Rogue and Monique were rescued, but Poncho died.

MY CAREER IN SALINA

Every year there are tragedies that happen during the holidays. Sometimes the tragedies are directly tied to the holidays.

Homes are decorated with electrical lighting and aroma pots. The extra load on electrical circuits is sometimes more than the system can handle. Some choose live Christmas trees that may or may not be fresh. There are videos that show the intense fire that a dry Christmas tree can create.

The hustle and bustle of the holidays can also lead to tragedy. Anyone who has children knows that a child left unattended can lead to trouble.

So, keep a close eye on children.
- Keep all flame producing items out of the reach of children.
- Keep dry trees out of your house.
- Keep extra electrical items to a minimum. Remember, it's always easier to prevent than to cure.

The investigation revealed that the three children started the fire in a closet with a lighter. Rogue and Monique were rescued, but Poncho died.

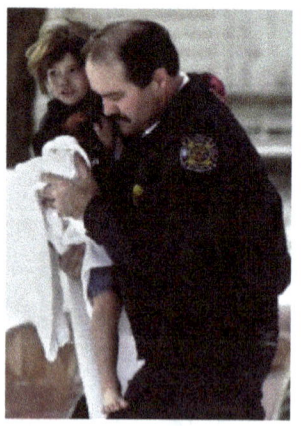

Every year there are tragedies that happen during the holidays. Sometimes the tragedies are directly tied to the holidays.

Homes are decorated with electrical lighting and aroma pots. The extra load on electrical circuits is sometimes more than the system can handle. Some choose live Christmas trees that may or may not be fresh. The public service videos show the intense fire that a dry Christmas tree can create.

The hustle and bustle of the holidays can also lead to tragedy. Anyone who has children knows that a child left unattended can lead to trouble.

So, keep a close eye on children.
- Keep all flame producing items out of the reach of children.
- Keep dry trees out of your house.
- Keep extra electrical items to a minimum.
- Remember, it's always easier to prevent than to cure.

THE MAN AND HIS LAUGH

At the end of our lives somebody, usually a religious person, stands before us and points out some "super special" things that we brought the world. It's a nice thing to do, but it's often a bit of an exaggeration. Yet on that rare occasion, it's no exaggeration at all.

His name was Gary Beach. He worked for 33 years at the Salina Fire Department. He was short in stature, a decent firefighter, and a good officer. He was also my officer for the better part of the first five years I spent with the SFD.

For most of us, our body's response to happiness is a smile. It's like a physiological connection exists between the heart and the lips. But, for Gary it went farther – much farther. For Gary the heart bone was connected to the smile bone and the smile bone was connected to the laugh bone. And it was a laugh like no other.

You need to start with a snapshot of his face to describe the laugh. The Riddler in the Batman movie – that's a close description. And with Gary the size of the smile was a direct indicator of what was to come.

Following the smile there were usually a few words – a comment – followed by a laugh that would instantly hit an octave level close to that of a peacock. Up and down, up and down, comments followed by laughter, comments followed by laughter.

Gary would already be in the "super special" category if this was where it stopped, but it didn't. Occasionally, Gary's laughter would catapult into what would best be described as a "Grand Mal Laugh". It would go on, and on, and on, and …

As it endured you honestly wondered if he would become anoxic and pass out from lack of oxygen. Sometimes, you would discover that you too were holding your breath. Slowly but surely, everyone would be laughing.

We try to understand why the "super special" folks like Gary are taken from us all too soon. With Gary I think it's clear. The Lord simply needed his laughter in Heaven.

P.S. Lieutenant Beach – thank you for being a role model to me during the most formative years of my career. I can't ever remember you coming to work in a bad mood – even on the dimmest of days. You were much more than a supervisor – you were more like a father figure. I'll never forget you.

ST. JOHN MILITARY SCHOOL

It was a beautiful fall day, not a cloud in the sky. I had a total of two months on as a Salina firefighter when the alarm sounded. We had a fire at the nostalgic St. Johns' Military School on Santa Fe.

I was stationed at station 1, so we would be the first to arrive. I quickly donned my hand-me-down fire coat and then stepped into my black rubber boots, pulling them up to my crotch. Next, I placed my yellow helmet. Lastly, I grabbed the shiny pull bar to help me with the step upwards onto the tailboard.

The driver sounded our siren and activated our emergency lights as we vacated the fire station. The great thing about riding on the tailboard of the fire truck is you get to see the burning structure and smell the smoke.

As we exited the fire station and headed north, you could see smoke off in the distance. We arrived in short order as the second on scene.

Story by Fire Lieutenant Tom Girard

The St. John's fire was truly one of my fire calls that stays with me. I was Lieutenant on Engine One with Keith Teasley as my driver.

When we arrived, there was heavy smoke on the third floor, with one room fully involved. Ken Giersch and I advanced a house line down the hallway when it got caught in a steam radiator. We were wearing 15-minute Scott air packs and were low on air.

I threw my light out the window allowing the outside crews to know we were in trouble. They hit the fire room with a heavy stream, allowing us to escape down the back stairs.

Close one for sure. I carried a piece of rope in my coat from that day on.

Captain McCabe was the shift commander and got involved in an accident at Ohio and Iron, on his way to the call.

The building was a total loss, but we had no serious injuries on the call.

A SPECIAL PETITION

A good friend of mine is facing a formidable foe by the name "Tobacco." Few take on this opponent without an incredible battle. The person has sought support via Facebook, so I decided to share a tobacco story. Here's that story.

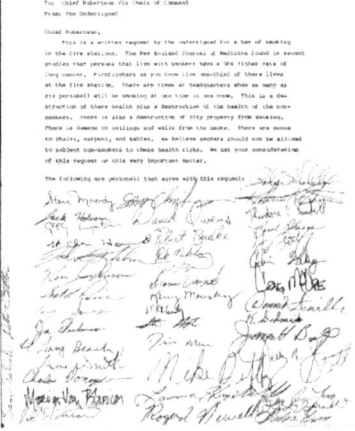

Like many, I gave old man Tobacco a try as a youngster. After several inhalations, I nearly lost my lunch. Maybe that's the secret to avoiding the old man, but he would get me in another way – for a while.

Firefighters get a bit nervous while sitting in the fire station waiting for the next call. Years ago – when I was a new firefighter – the common way to relieve that tension was Tobacco. Six of every ten Salina firefighters were smokers and there was no place in the fire station where you couldn't light up – including the kitchen table.

I was one of the four in ten non-users, but it's fair to say that second-hand smoke had me taking in around a half-pack a day. A drive to work one morning changed things.

A radio national news reporter talked about a medical study that had recently been published in the New England Journal of Medicine. The study documented the adverse effects of second-hand smoke. I immediately recognized my opportunity.

I decided to write an anti-smoking petition. The petition asked for the entire fire station to be smoke free. It seemed like a good idea to ask for the whole and hope for a portion. Now you need to understand that this was the early 1980's – well before most buildings had smoking restrictions. The City of Salina had none.

I got a big percentage of the firefighters to sign the petition – even smokers. To everyone's shock – including mine – the fire chief enacted my petition just as requested.

I was immediately about as popular as a diaper rash. Some eventually got over their hatred towards me, but some never did.

Over the years I have watched several of my friends go through the withdrawal process of smoking cessation. I quit smoking another way.

Addictions have a strangle hold on many people. We need to help those that want it – users and bystanders.

CRITICAL INCIDENT STRESS

Critical incident stress is a series of negative psychological and physiological reactions to a traumatic event. It occurs after a person has been exposed to a traumatic event. It occurs after a person has been exposed to or witnessed the event, which can be a line-of-duty death, a co-worker suicide, a multicausality incident, or delayed intervention.

Critical incident stress is a normal response to an abnormal event, and it varies from person to person.

Critical incident stress management is a selection and implementation of crisis intervention tactics to reduce the impact of the event, speed up the recovery process, and assess the need for further services.

There was no CISM program during most of my career with the SFD.

Personally, I have some doubts about having fellow workers with no professional degree conducting a program of such complexity. I watched medics handle stress in different ways. Some would resign.

Others that were vested in the retirement system would simply take early retirement. Some serious cases forced the medic to be committed to the hospital psychiatric ward.

Let me share, just a few stressful calls I had. You can then ask yourself, "How could anyone handle that stress?"

TRAIN INCIDENT

Dispatch: "Medic 1, respond to the railroad tracks on Iron St. by the Hilton Inn. We have a report of a subject that has been struck by a train."

Medic 1: On our arrival we found a middle-aged woman lying on the railroad tracks. Her legs were lying several feet away. She intended suicide by lying across the train tracks. The eerie thing was the lady was fully conscious. So, we had to treat and transport her.

One of the firefighters/EMTs had to pick up the legs and put them in the ambulance. She survived for around 20 minutes after our arrival at the hospital.

CHOKING CHILD

On this day there was 8-10 inches of snow on the ground and the roads were snow packed. I was assigned to Medic 2. And we were at the hospital, having transported another patient.

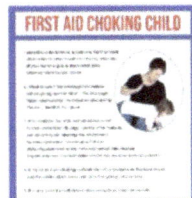

Dispatch: "Medic 2, respond to a residence for a child choking."

Medic 2: Our speed of response was slowed because of the snow-packed roadway. On arrival we were met by a father, standing on the porch holding a limp child.

The father handed the child to my partner, and we went directly to the ambulance. We administered first aid for a choking child. Simultaneously, we left the scene to go to the hospital. About halfway to the hospital, my partner got a return pulse. Then the child's breathing returned shortly after we got to the hospital. The mother and father were highly emotional – they were crying ecstatically, hugging my partner and me, and thanking us through deep sobbing.

Weeks later we heard the sad news. The child had gone too long without a pulse and without breathing. The result was severe brain damage. The child would never walk again, never speak again. I would occasionally see the child at the mall being pushed in a wheelchair, with her head strapped against the headdress of the wheelchair.

It hurt me deeply that we didn't get there fast enough. Every time I saw the boy, it brought back a sad memory. One that will never go away.

SPLIT RAIL FENCE

The young man was taking his buddies dads' super-charged Mustang for a cruise. Just as he kicked the car into its highest gear, directly across from Lakewood Lodge, the car fishtailed.

He then lost control of the car and it went down a steep embankment. The car rolled onto its 'top just as it hit the bottom of the embankment - at that same time striking a split-rail fence, driving one of the rails through the car's windshield.

The split-rail struck the young boy in a shearing angle, from the top of his forehead down to his chin. If the rail would've hit him squarely, he would've been killed instantly. On exam the place where the boy's nose would've been had two bubbly bleeding ports. Asked about complaints, the boy said he needed to blow his nose. We advised him to not to do that.

One of the boy's eyes was laying on the side of his head, with the other eye in its socket, but obviously injured too. We applied suction and oxygen by mask over the two nasal ports. He was extricated rapidly and transported to the hospital.

Outcome: The boy lost both of his eyes. He also had extensive facial repairs. But devasting as it was, there were no other injuries.

Last words: I would estimate that over my career there have been upwards of 50 calls that have permanently been seared, forever, into my memory. But I think several stories are enough examples to make my message. My purpose in telling these stories – "Understand what an FF/Medic goes through performing their job. And share your thanks when you get the chance.

Brad Burr and Jessica Goertzen provide two more personal stories to help make sure you get help if you need it.

CRITICAL INCIDENT STRESS

Retired FF/EMT Brad Burr

There are lots of things I would love to share. We all have our own stories. I was only in the game for 15 years. But over those years I experienced similar incidents.

A lot from when I worked for the Hutchinson Fire Department. And several others throughout the rest of my career at the Salina Fire Department. Mainly towards the end of my career. Obviously, that's when I had to give it up.

I've had cases where I have attempted suicide. I have been hospitalized as well. And I went to a 2-week inpatient/retreat in California for post-trauma stress. So, I always try to stay in touch and around the guys even currently. So, they know they always have someone to talk to.

Unfortunately, even then we lose some that we could've reached out to. Not just FD but law enforcement, dispatchers, volunteers and paid. All the first responders.

Had I had the proper CISD and back-up during my worst time, I probably would still be on the service. But maybe just in a different role.

But things happen for a reason. And I don't regret doing 15 strong years, even under circumstances of having to leave due to post traumatic stress syndrome.

CRITICAL INCIDENT STRESS

By Jessica Goertzen

I grew up in a medical household. My father is still a paramedic at the age of 76. It made perfect sense to me that I would fall in love with a firefighter/EMT.

I met John when he was at the Salina Fire Department for just 3 months. I had the opportunity to watch him grow in his career from being an EMT all the way to being a Battalion Chief. Listening to my father's stories encouraged me to become a nurse, which I have been for 20 years. Listening to the stories of John scared me, gave me anxiety, and worried for him. There are several calls that stand out to me over the 27 years. He would talk about a lot of his calls, because he knew that I could handle it since I was also in the medical field. He would also discuss calls with my father.

Early in his career, he went on a call with a SIDS baby who unfortunately did not survive. Once he went to a car accident, where he knew the relatives of the victim, and he found the victim in his front car seat, however his head was in the back seat. He went on a call where an elderly man had shot himself in his tub in his home and his wife found him. He called me one evening because he had just been on a call where a nurse that I worked with had committed suicide by hanging herself. He said that it was so eerie because she was still in her blue scrubs and clogs. He went on a call with my father in the country and found a toddler, deceased, sitting incorrectly in a car seat. He went on a call where there had been a domestic dispute, and the male had taken his life.

He would call and talk to me often about calls and we would work through them together. When we couldn't find a balance, or it was just too much for him, he would attend counseling, but he was never able to find a good fit for him in a therapist. He needed someone that was trained in this type of trauma. He tried different medications as well.

All through the bad calls and adversity, he continued to educate himself, be involved in many committees, give all of himself to his fire department and his men. He worked fearlessly and to the absolute best of his ability to help the fire department become everything that he knew it could be. He was committed to being the best Battalion Chief, leader, role model, and he was always available to his men. When a call didn't go right, a fireman was struggling with something, or an issue with being administrative personnel was weighing on him, he continued his commitment to the fire service.

There are so many emotions that come to mind about John and his 27-year fire department career. He was elated, honored and proud. He was also emotionally broken down and physically tired. I don't believe that there is enough emotional or mental assistance that can be provided to fire department personnel. There should be a constant check-in situation with each of them and checking in with each other. There should be no fear in saying that you need help.

I will never know the exact reason, but my fireman, John Goertzen, chose to take his life on March 17, 2023, in our home, and I was the one who found him. There is nothing that will ever erase that image for me, and there is nothing else that I can do for him except bring greater awareness and acceptance of mental health.

I share John's story in the hope that if you are struggling, you are encouraged to ask for help.

Jessica and Brad, Thank you for sharing your stories. I hope the department purchases a copy of this book for each of the firefighters. And all Firefighter/Medics will forever read your stories and follow your advice.

ST. JOHNS BAPTIST CHURCH

It was early evening, not yet dark, when the alarm sounded.

"Heavy smoke and flames showing from St.Johns Baptist Church on north 9th."

The brick church was so close to fire station 1 that you could've ran to it on foot – less than ½ a block.

The rest of this story is writtn by FF/Medic Jerry Short & Lt, Willis Sutton.

FF/MEDIC JERRY SHORT

I believe this happened on November 29th of 1999. I might have the date wrong as it's been a minute. My recount of the night might be a little foggy as well but as I remember that is how I will tell my story of how it went down.

I was the paramedic on M-1 that evening and don't exactly remember who my partner was that night. Responding to the church that was just a block away so very little time to come up with a game plan enroute.

I remember that James Forsey was the tailboard on E-1 and Larry Hemphill was the officer. Greg Brockway was acting Driver. When we pulled up there were flames shooting out the back of the church. The flames were blue in color, so we knew that it was being fed by a gas line. James wasn't ready and I had jumped out of the medic unit and suited up right away. I grabbed an air pack off E-1 and then went to the back of the truck and pulled a 2" line to the southeast window of the basement.

When Larry got to the window and the line was charged, we broke the window and went inside. As soon as we made it closer to the fire, I opened the nozzle and the hose went limp, I tried opening and closing the nozzle to try and water hammer any kinks out with no luck. I dropped the line and started chasing the line out to see if I could find any kinks. Larry exited the basement with me, and he went to the pump panel to see if he could see what was going on with the pump.

Larry brought the hose out with him. He was able to get the pump running properly and I tested the flow in the hose. We had plenty of pressure. I was standing between a van and the church building. And, I was yelling at Larry, saying "We are good, let's go!" All the sudden there was an explosion and all I could see was a huge brown and orange glow,

I couldn't see anything else and as if in slow motion I turned to run. I started getting pummeled with bricks and knocked to the ground. My ears were ringing, and it was very silent for a few seconds. I remember hearing that a firefighter was missing and possibly trapped in the building.

My hands were pinned, and I could not get to my radio. As I was lying there, I started to try and control my breathing and struggled a little to free my right hand. I needed to get it loose for two reasons. The main reason was to be able to remove my mask if I ran out of air. I would have suffocated if I wasn't able to take my mask off after running out of air.

The second reason was to call out Mayday. I needed to reach my radio and let them know my location. I remember lying in the pile of rubble and seeing flames going over the top of me and getting soaked with water at the same time. I was finally able to free my right hand enough to get to my radio.

It was not long before I could hear and feel my brother's moving bricks and clearing debris to get me out of there. If I remember correctly, I was only trapped for 14 minutes. Doesn't seem that long but I was scared to death. The whole time I was lying there not sure if I was going to get out seemed like forever. When they removed enough bricks to pull me out, we found out that my leg was pinned under a beam. We were able to get my leg free, but we lost a boot.

When they pulled me out, they wanted to rush me to a cot. I just remember saying "Give me a second to catch my breath." I just need to catch my breath for a second. Turns out that I was having trouble catching my breath due to a punctured lung. John Vishnefski put me in the back of the ambulance and hauled me to the hospital.

When I was in the ER the doctor wanted to put a chest tube in and I begged them not to. I had seen them put in before and I knew I didn't want any part of that. He agreed that we could wait and see what Berquist wanted to do. They agreed to just monitor it closely. I also remember Chief Girard in the ER telling Dr. Henson to do whatever it takes, whatever I need. Henson asked him if I was his son and Girard said "Yes, they are all my sons."

CHURCH FIRE

By Lieutenant Willis Sutton

My driver, Ron Green, firefighter Sarah Beem and I responded from Station 2 to a reported fire at St. John's Baptist Church. Engine 1 arrived and reported fire in the basement and car on fire beside the church. Engine 1 had laid a line into the parking lot of the church. Fire command requested that we stage at the hydrant at 9th and Bishop.

As we were going by the rear of the church, I noticed fire coming from the back of the church. I asked the command if we should lay a line to the back of the church. Command response was to stand by. Command, after a short pause, requested that we lay a line to the front and make entry to the 2nd floor.

We made the hydrant, and I had my firefighter pull the 2-inch line. I took an axe to take the glass out of the door to make entry. I was on air from the SCBA and waiting for my firefighter to be prepared before breaking the glass.

At that moment the explosion happened. It blew the doors of the church and me off the steps.

I remember sliding on my back on the SCBA. I got up and fire was then coming out of the front of the church. I helped my firefighter position the hose to the front of the church. I then went to the north side to check what happened.

The north side of the church was down and the house beside it was on fire. I didn't hear any radio traffic after that due to battery failure or damage. I then went to the south side to check on the crew working there. I located Lt. Hemphill in the parking lot and asked if everyone was accounted for, but Short was trapped under a pile of bricks.

I asked where and he took me to one of the vehicles that was up against the side of the church. I couldn't see much, and Lt. Hemphill started removing bricks. Fire was coming out of the side of the church that had been blown out. I noticed a large pile of brick, metal, and lentils on top of the car. I directed firefighter Forcey to go to the front of the church and get firefighter Beem with the 2-inch line and told him to protect me.

I then got on top of the car and removed the debris. Shortly thereafter Short was freed and we took him to the ambulance. After Short was transported, my firefighter and I then went to rehab. Joe Dickinson was the paramedic. When he was taking my vitals, he informed me that I had been burned. I had not felt that I had been burned. He told me I had some loose skin. I then looked at my fire hood and it had holes burned around where my SCBA was.

Firefighter Beem and I then left the ambulance which was staged at the front of the church. I noticed a line going into the front door and down the stairs inside. I tried to find out who was inside. Nobody knew.

I then started making short pulls on the line to get them out. It was Lt. Weese. He said it had been reported that a firefighter was trapped in the northeast corner. Firefighter Beem and I then sat on a monitor supplied by Engine 2, on the northwest corner of the building, till around midnight.

I then went to the hospital where they took care of my burns. I had a small 3rd degre4 burn to my right ear and ringing in my ears. Second degree burns around my face at points where my facemask didn't cover. Second degree burns around my wrists that my SCBA mask was heat checked and all the Velcro on my fire gear was melted.

The next day a hearing doctor said that I had damaged my right ear. And, I had some tone deafness.

COMMUNICATIONS

I always placed a high priority on recognizing the great things that my firefighters did.

Also, once I was appointed Deputy Chief, I wanted better communications from staff officers to the firefighters.

So, I started a monthly newsletter.

It was so popular firefighters would take a regular watch on the bulletin board for its 'posting.

I used this same communication tool when I went to be the Fire Chief in Leavenworth, Stafford County, and El Dorado.

TRUST YOUR GAUGES

An early morning fog set in on Saline County on October 11, 1985, as a Montana couple lifted off the Salina Municipal Airport runway in their single-engine airplane. Apparently, the pilot didn't think the fog would be a big problem since he was not only a pilot, but also an experienced pilot instructor. But a problem did occur.

Shortly after lift-off the pilot radioed back to the flight tower that he was having equipment difficulties and was returning to the airport. That was his last radio message.

Minutes later the 911 dispatch center received a call from a farmer who reported seeing an airplane crash into his field. Emergency crews responded to the scene to find the airplane had gone straight down into the ground – propelling the front of the aircraft several feet into the soft, wet soil. Both husband and wife were dead.

Investigators later theorized the pilot lost sight of the ground because of the fog and became disoriented. Instead of trusting his gauges, he went with what he thought was correct. As an instructor he certainly knew better.

You can't predict and plan for every scenario that might happen in an emergency, but not planning for those we can predict is a recipe for disaster. Yet, that's exactly what those of us in emergency operations often do. And we make all sorts of excuses for our failure. Here's a few.

"Emergencies are too varied to predict, you have to just go with your gut feeling." *"Written policies and procedures don't put out fires, firefighters put out fires."* Or maybe you've heard this one. *"We don't need policies; we just need to practice "simple common sense."*

To that last quote I would say, "It's not that simple and it's not that common."

So, what's my suggestion?

I would suggest that you break down your operations into as many categories and subcategories as you can think of. Then, schedule regular brainstorming sessions with your people to address each of these areas.

Define some clear, best practice, simple steps to each of these categories and subcategories. Pick your best writer and have them put the ideas down on paper. Those that are already written will only need tweaked. Once you've been through all the categories and subcategories, start over again. These brainstorming sessions should never stop.

Then – practice, practice, practice using them.

And, when the emergency comes – trust your gauges.

OTHER FIRSTS

I was one of three existing SFD Field EMTs.
I went on to complete my Bachelor's Degree from Kansas State University. I was also the first and only National Fire Academy Executive Fire Officer (4 - 2-week research driven programs).

SMOKY HILL RIVER RESCUE

The two young teens decided to have some good old-fashioned fun. The plan was to enter the Smoky Hill River on a small inflatable raft, then float into the city. For several reasons this was "one bad plan."

The months preceding this day had seen unprecedented rainfall. It rained so much the water control gates at Kanopolis Lake were opened full bore. The result was recording amounts of water flowing down the Smoky Hill River. What was usually a lazy river was now a raging river.

Next reason this was a bad plan was the raft size. Their choice was the equivalent of riding a tricycle on Interstate 70 – clearly an undersized ride.

One last reason was the ambient temperature. It was cold enough that the boys donned jackets – warm jackets. Unfortunately, they failed to add flotation jackets.

The ride down the river was uneventful until they hit the rapids. The rapids immediately flipped the toy-sized raft like a pancake – tossing the boys into the frigid, boiling rapids. Awaiting the boys, a thousand feet ahead were scores of wedged cottonwood trees.

Boy One went to the left and was pulled under the tree wedge with the sucking power of a monstrous leech. Boy Two stayed mid-stream and was tossed up onto a tree pile like a rag doll. One boy dead and another almost dead – the results of "one bad plan."

The rescue team arrived to find the boy perched upon the trees in the middle of the raging river – only recognizable as a human when he moved. Adding to the difficulty of the rescue was the sixty-foot straight walls on each side of the river, coupled with the deafening noise of the roaring water.

Rescuer George Elliott – the guy with the most technical rescue knowledge – was the one summoned to the Command Post. A detailed plan was developed and drawn on a tablet. Afterwards, the plan was driven to the other side of the river to show other rescue team members. Paramedic George Elliott and EMT FF Were the two key ones to complete the lifesaving in the Smoky Hill River rescue.

A special gun blasted a string line across the river to pull the rescue rope. A flotation jacket was attached to a rope and floated into the boy. He would grab the vest, don it, and then be pulled from the death chute. That was the plan.

Unfortunately, the roar of the river didn't allow the "sharing of the plan" with the boy. After grabbing the jacket, he simply disconnected it from the rope. The plan would need to be modified.

Putting a rescuer in the water was the last thing the team wanted, but it was the only other choice besides leaving the boy. With a short tag line in hand, the rescue team lowered Rescuer Chad Scoville into the water and up to the boy. Chad quickly hooked into the boy and then gave the signal to the rescuers to hoist.

Minutes later the boy was safe on land.

This has been the most complex rescue witnessed in my thirty-seven-year career. The entire team deserves credit for the rescue, but special recognition must go to two of the rescuers – Chad and George.

Not many people would have volunteered to be dropped into the Smoky Hill River that day – even to rescue a young boy. What Chad did was as heroic as heroic gets.

Then there is George. He is a rescue genius like no other. He drew up "one good plan".

It was better than good – it was GREAT.

Chad Scoville

TRENCH COLLAPSE KILLS ONE

The company had been doing trench work along Crawford Street for upwards of a month. They reached the intersection of Santa Fe and things got more difficult.

A crisscrossing of different sized pipes traversed the hole that was dug. And the hole they dug was upwards of 20 feet deep by 100 feet wide.

This size of hole with pipes going different directions made shoring almost impossible. And to make things even more dangerous, traffic remained open right alongside the trench.

The company had some makeshift plywood panels placed in points where they felt it was needed. But the trench collapsed down through the plywood panels down upon two workers.

Firefighters arrived and found one worker buried up to his hips and a second worker was underneath one of the plywood panels with approximately 4 feet of dirt on top of the panel. It took around 30 minutes to free the partially covered worker. The second worker was another story.

It took over an hour to get to the second worker freed, who unfortunately had died before he was freed.

THE DEVIL'S IN THE DETAILS

*Everyone makes mistakes and hopefully we learn through those mistakes. The great thing is mistakes learning is just as valuable when we learn from the mistakes of others. Here's one of my mistakes to remind you that "The Devil's in the Details.

Something unexpected happened when the SFD Fire Marshal retired. Instead of promoting a replacement, the Deputy Chief absorbed the duties – me being the Deputy.

Three Inspectors and a Public Educator would ensure that my lack of a prevention background wouldn't lead to a catastrophe. Or would they?

The City of Salina has the Smoky Hill River Festival each spring during the first week of June. Planning for the festival is almost non-stop, so it wasn't unusual to meet with organizers in early January.

During the organizational meeting the group discussed a burn display by a California artist. We were told, "The details will follow."

Five months later an Inspector walked into my office. With a look of shock upon his face he asked me, "Have you seen the gigantic "Ring of Fire" prop over at the Smoky Hill River Festival?" He went on to explain the enormity of the prop.

"It's like the world's biggest doughnut! Before they stuffed the chicken wire frame structure with straw you could've held dune buggy races in it. And as we speak the Californians are dousing the straw with diesel fuel."

A good Fire Marshal would've followed up long ago to get the "details that didn't follow." So, what to do now? It was too late to simply cancel.

Mother Nature pitched in with heavy winds that night. I was like an umpire calling the game on account of lightning – and about as popular. The game would take place the next day – during daylight.

That next day we sent over enough waterpower to put out the "Great Chicago Fire." Two pumpers and one aerial truck – all connected to fire- hydrant water supply. At any moment the firefighters could have instantly turned the Ring of Fire into Noah's Ark.

At the city staff meeting the following week festival organizer Martha brought me a token reminder – a cupcake with burning candles. It left an everlasting impression.

Whenever I see a cupcake, I remind myself, "The Devil's in the Details."

CO DISASTER DIVERSION

Story by SFD Medic Mike Duffy

As I recall, the family had just gotten to the pool. The boy arrived a few minutes before the family.

So, his exposure was longer. They were there less than 15 minutes.

The boy was out of the pool and just collapsed.

When I arrived, the mother, daughter, and the boy were sitting in the lounge waiting for us.

When I walked in, I noticed all three were scared looking  and quiet. I asked the mom what happened. She said they had been at the pool only 15 minutes when the boy collapsed and was unconscious for several seconds.

For some reason, I don't know why, probably training by Training Chief Gale Aills, I thought of CO carbon monoxide. So, I asked the daughter "Do you have a headache?" She said "Yes, I do." I asked the mother too. She said, "Yes, I do have a bad one."

I told my partner, and a ride-along medic, to get vital signs on all 3. I went to the manager and asked, "Do you have any gas appliances?" She said "Yes, water heaters." I asked her where, and she said it was next to  the pool. I asked him to show me. He showed me a door next to the pool with a large gap at the bottom.

My CO detector was in the shop, so I called for Engine 1 to respond to the scene. This only took a couple minutes. The manager had a cow and said "No, no fire truck!" I told her it would be okay that there wouldn't be a charge to check for CO and would want to be safe.

Engine 1 officer Lt. Craig McCabe's meter went off outside.

I had the whole family now, with dad, in the ambulance, and all on oxygen by mask.

McCabe's meter read 1600 ppm in the pool, 600 in the lobby, 400 on the 3rd floor. None of the other guests were symptomatic. The fire crew ventilated the motel. Some stayed, some went to another motel.

The source of the CO was a plugged-up flu, on the water heater, in the pool room.

My comment: I believe Mike is much too humble about this emergency.

Only a few paramedics would've solved the problem that was causing the illness with the family. Especially, so quickly.

What could have caused catastrophic consequences didn't happen because of a very sharp thinking paramedic. Great job SFD Paramedic Mike Duffy.

DEAD MAN'S CURVE

East of Salina, Kansas there is an "S" curve on Old Highway 40. It appears the farmhouse on the curve's eastern lead-in was the design agent. The highway was built back in the day when a single property owner had strong rights – beyond everyone traveling down the road in the future.

Nobody knows when or who coined the nickname, but we can easily guess why this stretch of Highway 40 was given the name – "Dead Man's Curve." And most Salina medics got to see the why firsthand.

My experience happened late one night in the fall of 1989. My partner and I were dispatched to the curve for a vehicle that rolled multiple times and was resting on its top out in the field.

A deputy sheriff met us when we stepped out of our ambulance. She told us there was one with no injury sitting on the edge of the roadway, and a second person was under the vehicle. He was supposedly dead.

I directed my partner to the non-injury patient while I worked my way through the soft plowed field to the dead subject. My flashlight's beam led me to the far side of the capsized '67 Ford Falcon. This was where the patient's head protruded from under the roof.

The face was turned rightwards. Skin was a light shade of K-State purple. As I took in the grisly sight, the unexpected happened – he gasped. I radioed my partner and the incoming rescue team about the new finding – code red, not code black.

The next radio message was to the emergency room physician to secure a "Do Not Resuscitate" orders in case we couldn't quickly get the patient freed – knowing our rescue truck's speed was like a turtle stampeding through peanut butter.

Conventional wisdom would dictate air bags be slid under the car to lift it off the patient. The problem was it took a bit of time to get the equipment set up and activated – and the patient was no longer gasping.

I looked at the little Falcon and decided to save time, we would skip the air bags and simply lift the car off the patient. If the decision was right, we would give the patient a better chance. If the decision was wrong, we would be calling Ryan's Mortuary.

The rescue team arrived and quickly made it to the car. Two rescuers squatted beside the patient ready to slide the patient out, while the rest of us positioned our hands under the edge of the roof top. On the count of "3" – we hoisted.

Up came the Falcon and out slid the patient. It was as simple as that. After a couple minutes of rescue breathing the patient's own respiratory drive kicked in. The patient survived.

So, what can we take away from this experience?

- First, it never hurts to double check important matters – another look, especially by someone more specialized in the matter, is a good practice.
- Get guidance from higher authorities if possible. A quick call to a higher authority helps ensure your choice and bolster confidence.
- Be willing to think outside the box. Standard procedures are great and should be the norm. But sometimes the result of following them is a dead patient.
- This incident had a great outcome, but don't judge yourself too harshly if that isn't the result. Bad results don't always mean poor choices. Sometimes it just wasn't meant to be.

Simplified, it means asking the right questions, making the right choices, and luck.

TERRY VAGUE – A FACE TO SAFETY

The year was 1973. This was Terry Vague's sophomore year at Salina Central High School – two years away from graduation and a full life ahead. So, it seemed.

Terry and I were in the same wood shop class – a classroom staged with big square wooden drawing tables at the front of the room and the work area with power saws in the back. There was no wall separating the two.

It was me and Terry and a few others that day – sitting at our drawing tables. Terry had his back to the power saw area, and I was facing it.

A couple other classmates were working in the power saw area. They were getting ready to run a rough cut two-inch thick piece of walnut through the table saw. The kick-back guard on table saws can be a pain in the neck, so this one had been removed.

As the students started to push the walnut board into the blade, it resisted. And in the blink of an eye the board was launched from the saw. The board flew thirty feet through the air where it struck Terry in the back of the head. Terry was killed instantly.

I've witnessed several lives lost from safety short-cuts during my lengthy emergency service career. There's always a strong safety response after the accident. Safety at once becomes paramount. But it never brings back those lost.

Flash forward to this past weekend in Stafford County. We had a farmer that decided they didn't need to follow the open burn policy. The person burned without calling into dispatch and they also burned at night – both clear violations.

The fire department responded to the illegal fire and extinguished it. Nobody got hurt or killed. But that doesn't mean there wasn't any danger. The reason it's illegal is "IT IS NOT SAFE!"

How many boards were pushed through that Salina Central High School guard-less table saw before the deadly one? Hundreds, maybe thousands. But that didn't make it safe.

Firefighting is an inherently dangerous occupation. But we don't need to do things to make it more dangerous.

Terry Vague and many others didn't have to die – and we shouldn't need more lost lives to learn the lesson.

A FIRE CHIEF'S WORST THING

What's the *worst thing* a fire chief could experience?

There are several things that come to mind. How about getting fired? The pink slip experience is certainly not a fun-filled event, but there's something that's worse, much worse.

How about a major fire at the home of the City Manager's best friend – and the fire department doesn't initially respond? That's a bad thing and a future story. But there's still something that's worse.

No, the **GRANDDADDY WORST EVENT** for a fire chief is hands down *"a serious injury or death of a firefighter"* – one of your firefighters.

It was a day that leading in didn't have any particular significance. So much so that details leading up to the event don't immediately come to mind.

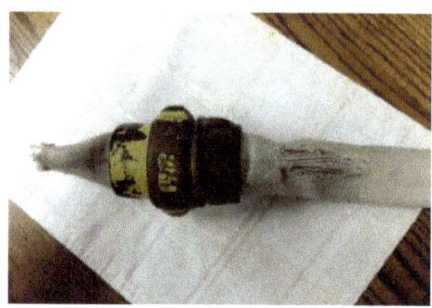

One recalls that a firefighter wanted to learn pumping operations. The crew decided to get some hose tested during the training. It wasn't uncommon – at this time in the department's history – to test a fire hose with an engine, especially when there wasn't much hose to test. And that was the case.

The hose was all laid out and the test started. As firefighters observed the hose, they noticed a few of the couplings were leaking. Instead of shutting down the engine while the couplings were tightened – which is what should've been done – firefighters simply started tightening the problem connections.

David was one of the firefighters. He had tightened several couplings when he came to another. This one was an old school solid brass coupling. The thick beast should have been retired and sold off for scrap, but it kept passing the muster. And today it just would not seal.

It would take a little more effort. David placed the spanners on the couplings with his head positioned directly above at exactly the time the trainee flipped the switch – the volume to pressure switch.

The extra surge was all that was needed to push a weak spot in the hose beyond its breaking point. Unfortunately, the bursting point in all the hose laid out was immediately adjacent to the coupling David was tightening.

The hose shot upwards like a rocket into David's head. The blow rendered him unconscious while dropping him to the pavement. Fellow firefighters were at his side practically seconds after it happened. In breakneck speed they treated, packaged, and transported him to the hospital.

David spent several days in intensive care before we got the best news a fire chief would ever get in his career – a severely injured would recover.

THE OLD DAYS
In Remembrance of Salina Fire Engineer Richard "Steve" Funke

When I tell emergency responders about the "old days" they often look at me with disbelief. Granted, there are only a few of us old dinosaurs left.

We started our career when air packs were optional. And there were only a few available – 15-minute sling-pack demand style.

There were no thermal cameras. No hoods. No sit-down seat for firefighters.

We rode on the tailboard with the wind blowing in our face, hanging on for dear life to a chin high chrome bar. On snowy days we might hook up a couple spanner belts and do a little skiing on the way back to the station. *"Old days"*

The gloves were the mustard-colored cotton jersey version. Medical gloves weren't available because infection control hadn't been invented yet. Mobile radios were just making their entry. Turnout gear resembled a heavy raincoat with thigh level rubber boots. "Old days"

I could have referred to the old days as the *"good old days"*, but we know that operationally it wasn't good. What was good though was the camaraderie.

During the *"old days"* emergency responders had a tighter bond. I believe it might best be explained with an example.

Several weeks ago, one of the old timers left us. His name was Richard "Steve" Funke. Many of us simply called him *"Mother."*

Mother spent much of his career as a fire engineer for the Salina Fire Department. And that role was probably part of the reason for the name *"Mother"*, but there was more, much more.

You see the caring didn't start or stop on the fire ground. It was constant, whether it was preparing meals, or just general concern for your welfare. That was Steve. We will miss him.

The *"old days"* – they weren't all bad.

WHO PACKS YOUR PARACHUTE?

The shortest distance between two objects is a straight line. That's the way the two medics saw it as they headed their ambulance toward the rural medical emergency. The only problem was this path was seldom traveled and mostly dirt road. That may have been why they didn't see the **"Low Water Crossing"** sign.

After the ambulance came to rest on the far side of the crossing – without its front wheels – the department called the fix-it guy – Master Mechanic Glen Wendt.

Glen recently concluded a career of over two decades as the Master Mechanic for the Salina Fire Department. He is truly an amazing mechanic, and moreover an amazing man.

The role that emergency personnel perform is worthy of the hero title, but what about their support crew? How great would any firefighter be if he was all dressed up in his turnout gear and his fire truck wouldn't move? He would be like a Dead Atheist – all dressed up and with no place to go.

Day in and day out Glen kept the machines running – vehicles, radios, lights, air packs, extinguishers, the list goes on and on.

Heroes can be demanding. That's to be expected when lives are at stake, but that doesn't make it any easier for those getting the demands. The expectations of the support crew can sometimes be greater than those placed upon the heroes. And the support folks don't get the glory.

Machines are used in every emergency. During his time the machines always worked. And he was the reason why. In my book that makes Glen Wendt a hero. Many times, over.

Congratulations on a great career!

THE SECRET OF LIFE

"Do you know the secret of life? It's "one thing" – just one thing. You stick to that, and the rest don't mean shit. What's the one thing? That's what you must find out."

Those are lines from the movie City Slickers when old-time Cowboy Curly is life counseling City Slicker Mitch.

This year was my 45th wedding anniversary and I served 37 years in emergency service before having to resign because of health problems. I must have done some things right to thrive for this long in two challenging ventures. So, if I had to boil it down – like Curly – to one thing, what would that one thing be?

It would be "harmony."

The definition of harmony that I like best is – "A combination of sounds considered pleasing to the ear." This musical definition is one that can apply to every situation – the smallest to the largest, the least fortunate to most fortunate.

Music is something that you can produce with the smallest of resources to the grandest. You can have a full orchestra accompaniment, or you can sing a duet with no instruments at all.

Somebody famous once said, "If you can't be happy with what you have, how could you be happy with more?" To me what this means is happiness should be happening all through during your trip. You won't have much fun – possibly none – if happiness doesn't come until you reach some grand attainment.

Strive for harmony. Harmony will bring happiness.

WHO'S GONNA FILL HIS SHOES?

He wasn't the typical "new guy" when he came to the Salina Fire Department twenty-five years ago. No, this was a seasoned professional – a Director of EMS beforehand. His name was George.

As the medical shift one supervisor, I had the distinct pleasure of having George as my new employee. George was also in paramedic school when he arrived and there was never an easier one to oversee.

The only mistake I can recall this perfectionist ever made wasn't a medical mistake at all – it was a cooking mistake.

George was the cook for the month and one evening he cooked up a batch of spaghetti. The problem was he put a few too many bags of uncooked spaghetti into the monster aluminum pot. As it grew, and grew, and grew – George frantically scraped off the overflow like a sailor scraping water off the deck of a mighty ship.

Another George recently left us – not through retirement but through death. His name was George Jones. He sang a song that – with some slight modification – is a perfect fit for George Elliott.

PITTSBURGH PLATE GLASS BUILDING FIRE

Story by Lieutenant Willis Sutton

January 7, 1980

Around 10:30 one evening, while I was getting ready for bed, an alarm came in for the 200-block east Iron. It was the Pittsburgh Plate Glass Building that was on fire. The response was Engine one, Ladder one and Ladder two. Ladder two was a 1949 open cab LaFrance. When we arrived, the building was charged with smoke.

A police officer had found a rear door open and smoke coming from it. I was the driver of engine one. We laid a 5-inch line from 5th and Iron to the front of the building. Ladder one staged on 5th street at the hydrant just south of Iron St. Ladder two was staged on 4th street. The crew, led by Lt. Leland Tinkler, took a line into the rear door off the alley. After working inside for a while, the front overhead door was opened, and the smoke had changed to a gray color. They asked for an exhaust fan to be set up, which I hung off the overhead door. The crew continued to work inside checking for extension. About that time, I looked at my watch and thought to myself, we should be cleaned up in bed by midnight.

Then a large puff of black smoke came out of the upper floor of the building with the truck parallel to Iron Street. Lt. Sanchez and FF Smith made onto the roof to ventilate. As soon as they opened the roof, a fire erupted and the roof started to sag.

The crew rushed to get off the roof. Engine one used its deck gun and Ladder one used its ladder nozzle to apply water to the open roof. The crew inside retreated to the exterior. A call back was enacted. The roof crew was making its way down the ladder to get off the roof. At that time the wooden wheel chalks were washed away by water that was running down the curb. The ladder truck rolled forward off its out-riggers. That brought the ladder down upon the building stopping its fall.

The truck rolled forward off its out rigors. That brought the ladder down upon building stopping its fall. The ladder just missing the large electrical transformer mounted on poles in the alley. The roof crew made it off the ladder and reposition it off the ladder and reposition it to supply water to the roof.

Engine one had every line pulled off it. I connected the steamer connection on the front of the truck to a hydrant in front of the truck to a hydrant in front of the building for more water. We laddered the front to knock out glass block windows then get water on the second floor.

I rescued the exhaust fan and pumped the truck until 7 a.m. At that time, we shut down the truck until we could get more fuel, because it was below an 1/8 of a tank. The next shift took over with the clean-up.

"WHO'S GONNA FILL THEIR SHOES"

The world is filled with emergency responders.
But just a few are chosen to tear your heart out when they perform. Imagine life without them."

No, there will never be another – stone-haired medic. A man in a more crisp uniform.
Lord I wonder – who's gonna fill their shoes?

God Bless the boys from the SFD. Pawnshop Rick and Junkyard Hank Much too soon their careers ended.

They tore up the eighties and nineties.
A bunch of Tom's and a Brock
And old Kenny G still echoes through the years

You know the heart of emergency service
Still beats in scrappy BK

You can tell when they sounded their siren and
lights Old Moose, Joe, and Jerry

Why I can feel them right here with me
On this Red Eagle rolling through the night

Who's gonna fill their shoes
Who's gonna stand that tall

Who's gonna play the accident scene
And the medical Cannonball

Who's gonna give their heart and soul To get to me and you
Lord I wonder, who's gonna fill their shoes
Yes I do wonder, who's gonna fill his shoes?

4-DOOR PLYMOUTH BELVEDERE

The year was 1977. It's funny how old memories sometimes pop into your head for no reason.

My meager savings were nearly exhausted after attending two years of college. This was back when running up a tab wasn't part of the college attendance formula. Not only was my college fund exhausted, so was my 1965 Ford Mustang.

I needed some wheels. I checked out the periodicals and there it was: "The Shopper's Guide" "1966 4-door Plymouth Belvedere II – low mileage – one-owner –$500 or best offer."

I called the number listed and arranged a time to look at the car – immediately. The owner turned out to be a female senior citizen. Even though the car was immaculate, it was a little old lady car.

The slant 6-cylinder engine was so quiet you couldn't even tell it was running – not a hot rod.

It was a living room wall beige color – not too striking. And it did indeed have four doors – not exactly a chick magnet. But it was perfect in another way – price. SOLD!

So, why did the Belvedere memory spring forth? I knew the answer after just a moment – it was the lessons. Belvedere's reliability was one lesson. Even though he wasn't the flashiest fellow on the block, he never failed me – even on the coldest Kansas morning. There are few things as important in life as reliability.

The immaculate condition of the car was another lesson. Belvedere was eleven years old and looked like he had just come off the showroom floor. A little old lady could keep a car pristine – shouldn't any young person be able to do the same?

Economy was the third lesson. Fuel consumption wasn't a big concern in the '70's but Belvedere was different – he was ahead of his time. Is my ultra conservative nature tied to Belvedere's lesson?

But the most important lesson of all was trust. There's something that's certain when a woman chooses a man that drives a four door Belvedere – she doesn't love him for his money or his status. Belvedere gave me and my high school sweetheart a ride to the cathedral for our marriage vows.

Memories of a 4-Door Plymouth Belvedere II weren't really all that strange after all.

HURRICANE KATRINA

Hurricane Katrina caused widespread devastation to the entire Gulf Coast of the United States in the first week of 2005.

The Federal Emergency Management Agency immediately sent out a call for help – 1,000 two-person fire crews.

Salina Fire Department Engineer David Turner and I volunteered.

We were notified Tuesday morning that we were needed, and by late Tuesday afternoon, we were in Wichita, ready to board a plane for Atlanta.

I told the Salina Journal, "I think it's our responsibility, in the fire service, that when they ask for help that we provide help."

We flew out of Wichita spending one day in Atlanta training, then serving 30 days in Mississippi along the Gulf Coast.

Mainly, we distributed information to those needing assistance with their losses. Two other Salina Fire Department members followed David and I serving another 30 days. The experience was memorable and brought a greater understanding of how to handle the need for help should we ever need it in Salina.

SALINA FIRE MARSHAL JERRY SCOTT

I served 28 years with the Salina Fire Department. A big share of those years was spent with a fire service icon named Jerry Scott.

Jerry spent most of his three decades with the Salina Fire Department in the Prevention Bureau.

Because he was a big, strong man he could have stayed in the main division of the department – the Firefighting Division. And he would have done well there.

But I believe Jerry spent most of his career in the Prevention Bureau because he could see the impact of the Prevention Bureau. Most of his years were also spent as the Fire Marshal.

Behind Jerry's leadership the Salina Fire Department became a nationally known Prevention Bureau. It is what it is today, because of what Jerry did back then.

Firefighting is an inherently dangerous occupation. The firefighter deaths at the World Trade Center clearly showed us that in extreme. But a Prevention Bureau, through an Inspection component, makes firefighting less dangerous. What you have without a good Inspection program is terrible dangers existing in buildings.

Public education is another lifesaving component of the Prevention Bureau. For most of Jerry's career, Salina and Lawrence were the only two fire departments in Kansas who had a non-firefighter full time Public Educator. Without a school Public Education program, too many children start fires, and some lose their life.

Prevention officers also excel at telling a fire's story and taking photos during fire investigation. Retired SFD EMS Chief Greg Brockway and I wrote a Salina Fire Department history book many years ago.

While doing the research for the book, we discovered that most of the information we found was pictures and documents put together by the Prevention Bureau.

Jerry was a man that always had a smile on his face. And I'm quite sure Jerry enjoyed every day of his life. I also had the pleasure of working with the man.

Preventing fires, stopping what could've been, makes Jerry a lifesaving hero many times over. Rest in peace Jerry, knowing the great impact you had on the Citizens of Salina.

NINETEEN RETIREES AT FM JERRY SCOTT'S FUNERAL SERVICE

A GOLFER'S FINAL WISH

It was a beautiful fall day, perfect for just about anything, especially a round of golf. The team of retired buddies met as usual in the clubhouse. After a quick check-in, they walked outside, stepped into their electric carts, and rode off towards *Hole #1*.

The round started as usual with friendly banter back and forth. Bob wasn't quite as talkative this morning, but it wasn't enough to be noticeable. This was the situation until they were on their way back towards the clubhouse on the back nine. That was when Bob made a few comments about not feeling well.

By this time, he didn't look too well either. So, the group decided it was best to call it a day and get Bob back to the clubhouse. They almost

made it back when it happened. Bob quit talking and went limp.

The dispatcher gave the short message – *"Subject down at the golf course – unknown disposition."* What seemed like eternity was a mere couple of minutes before our arrival. We wheeled our ambulance cart and equipment over to Bob.

The quick-look paddles positioned on the chest showed ventricular fibrillation. I reached over to the monitor, turned the dial to 200 joules, pushed the charge button, and re positioned the paddles on the chest. I shouted – Clear, Clear, Clear – then pressed the two red paddle buttons to send the shock.

Again, I looked at the monitor screen. It changed. The monitor now showed a livable rhythm and Bob had a pulse. Immediately, I felt a surge myself – a surge of pride. Death had been postponed for the moment. I was a lifesaver!

It was about this time that one of Bob's buddies turned to another friend and made a comment I have never forgotten. "Remember what Bob always told us?", *"I pray that when I die – it's on the golf course."*

It hit me like a cup of Colombian coffee. I instantly went from "Hero to Goat" in a millisecond. I just fouled up this poor fellow's last final

wish on earth. Bob never regained consciousness and died three days later in ICU.

I have had over twenty-five years to think about that day on the golf course. Hopefully, Bob and I will get to talk one day.

The reason for me sharing this story is so you understand how vitally important it is to have a legally signed plan for what to do at the end of your life. You must carry a copy with you so somebody can present it to EMS personnel if they are accidentally called. And be sure that all the right people know about the plan.

Don't let a paramedic mess up "The End."

*Bob was not the real name of the person in this story.

NOT A BUCKET LIST
My youngest son writes a blog of letters to his daughter called – "Letters to Amaia". I thought you might enjoy this one and got his permission to pass it along.

Dear Amaia,

You are now almost 7 months old, and you have come so far. It seems like just yesterday I held you in my arms for the first time and you struggled to move your arms and open your eyes. Now you are crawling, smiling, and laughing. Time is not stopping. You are growing every day, and it makes me think of the bright future you have.

The other day I was watching the movie "The Bucket List". It struck a thought in my head about the life I have lived and the things I have done in my life. I want you to live your life with no regrets and never be afraid of failure. In the movie two friends decided to live their last days to the fullest by making a list of things they wanted to do before they died. The lesson learned from this movie was that time machines do not exist. I cannot go back to read you a book that I didn't because I was too tired. I cannot go back and write you these letters.

Recently, I sat down and wrote a list. This is not a bucket list, but a life list. I call it a life list because we shouldn't do these things because we fear death, but that we embrace life with a zeal that God created us to possess. One of my favorite quotes by Henry David Thoreau paints my message perfectly so that you will live your life free of regret. "Never look back unless you plan on going that way."

SFD FF/MEDIC/RN GREGORY COMPTON
The SFD Salina Fire Department lost a third member of the department within a short period of time. His name was Greg Compton.
Greg didn't serve a long period of years with the department, but during his SFD career he had more impact than many others who served decades longer.

On the fun side, one retiree recalled, "Comp, as we called him, will be remembered by many for his famous saying "One Run-One Sandwich."

Paramedics and Firefighters have the most stressful jobs there are.

His one-to-one practice may have just been Greg's way of dealing with the stress on the job.

Greg was a firefighter, a paramedic, and a registered nurse. In response to his death there was a huge outpouring on social media, unlike any other, from those who shared time with Greg. Many said "he made everyone smile and laugh. Another said he was "one of the good guys."

Fun was what he made of work. Numerous said he was always happy and made everyone smile. You could come to work feeling down and within 10 seconds he would have you laughing, and your spirits would be great.

And then there was Greg's world-famous black Lab named Bo. Comp taught Bo the great skill of fetching him a beer from the cooler. But not all Bo's skills were good. Bo's hunger pangs made all food within reach at risk. One Thanksgiving, Bo consumed the Thanksgiving turkey, plus a few holiday pies.

Bo was also famous for being the only dog to take several ambulance rides. What happened was Bo was always getting loose from the back yard. The animal shelter folks knew Bo and wouldn't pick him up if Greg put him back in the yard. It just so happened that several times Bo got loose when Greg was on duty. Hence, a short ambulance ride.

But don't be fooled by Greg's having fun at work. Behind that funniness was a highly intelligent man, one who knew when to turn the "funny switch." off, and the serious switch on.

Many said Greg's "medical knowledge and skills were unmatched. Those skills helped all the emergency crew members stay calm. Just like Greg.

On many of these calls the clock is ticking. If the emergency crew doesn't get the patient to the hospital in time, they sometimes die. There are some sights that FF/Medics, including Greg, will never erase from their mind. The lay public only sees a fraction of what the emergency crew sees.

I think it's "fair to say" that Comp lived a life like no other. There are only a few occupations that involve saving lives. Some people are alive today because of Greg. He was a true hero.

The fire alarm sounded when word of Greg's death was heard. Then, everyone's heart missed a beat. And, unfortunately, we know you can't unwring the bell.

So, I think what we should to do in Greg's memory is, "Have another drink and another sandwich."

THIRTY-ONE HEROES
PAYING LAST RESPECTS OF HERO GREG COMPTON

Thirty-one Emergency Service Professionals, plus others, gathered today at Ryan's Mortuary to pay their last respects for Paramedic/RN Greg Compton. The attendees came from far and near. Including Kansas City, Bonner Springs, and Missouri. Six of the crowd shared heart felt stories of what a wonderful man Greg was to work with. How he touaed the lives of his patients. How he touched so many hearts.

Above all else, how he was a true hero.

Left to Right – Greg Nicholson, Calvin Kelsey, Roger Newell, Jane Steen, Mick McCallum, Ken Giers/, Rob Pengra, unknown, unknown, Ron Householter, John Vishnevsky, Ernie Sanchez, Marvin VanBlaricon, Steve Moody, Lee Soldan, Willis Sutton, Ken Johnson, Mark Grosland, Monte Elam, Judy Piercy, Mike Davis, Rod Stack, Kevin Pahls, Mike Duffy, Tom Girard, Jim Weese, Scott Hawley, Jim Wittman, Keith Teasley, Jeff Rittel, and Chad Scoville.

SALINA FIRE DEPARTMENT - LOCAL 782

The Salina Fire Department has one of the oldest fire departments with a Union.

I served as one of three officers. The other two were Willis Sutton and Rick Nicholson.

We referred to ourselves as the "Three Amigos" after the Three Stooges.

We were three good friends too.

SALINA FIRE CHIEF TOM GIRARD

Chief Girard had a stellar career, serving in all the ranks except paramedic.

Records show that Chief Girard second longest tenure behind only Chief Travis.

He served during a tumultuous time with running the ambulance operations. I have serious doubt that without his leadership the ambulance operations would have been moved from the Salina Fire Department to a 3rd party private operation.

Nobody is perfect in every way and perfect to everyone. I rate him highly because during his tenure he allowed firefighters to take just about any training opportunity there was. And I attended as many as I could.

He allowed me to crossover from EMS Lieutenant to Fire Lieutenant. I explained that my desire in taking the Fire Lieutenant position was to get more fire operations experience to prepare me for future fire chief positions. He listened.

Girard also promoted me to Deputy Chief. Without the experience I attained from serving as Deputy Chief, I seriously doubt whether I would've ever made it to fire chief.

THE SALINA ENDING

I had a career plan that included the long-term goal of Fire Chief. So, I set goals of taking every educational opportunity I could find.

First, I finished my bachelor's degree at Kansas State University. Then, I took FF1&2, Fire Officer 1&2, Fire Investigator 1&2, Driver Operator, Hazardous Material Technician, Paramedic, KU Certified Public Manager, and then nine two- week National Fire Academy classes in Emmitsburg, Maryland.

The last four of the NFA classes were the 4 two-week classes named EFO Executive Fire Officer. It's the highest fire leadership class there is anywhere. It entails a minimum 30-page research paper after each 2-week class. The papers are reviewed by a college professor and must meet master's collegiate research standards.

Then there's job experience.

Along the way in my career, I served in every work position there was to serve. Firefighter, Fire Engineer, Paramedic, EMS Lieutenant, Fire Lieutenant, Deputy Chief., and Interim Fire Chief.

Therefore, with all the training and all the work positions I was highly marketable.

Unfortunately, I wasn't chosen to fill the Salina Fire Chief position. What hurt the most was the person chosen didn't have a fraction of the education and the work positions that I had. It was really their loss because they spent thousands of dollars training me.

To reach my goal I would have to leave Salina. This meant leaving a place where I had spent my whole life. But it would've been silly for me to give up on my grand goal.

So, I didn't.

After serving 28 years with the SFD, I tearfully said my goodbyes to my family and friends. And I took the Fire Chiefs job in Leavenworth, Kansas.

CHAPTER 3
MY CAREER IN LEAVENWORTH

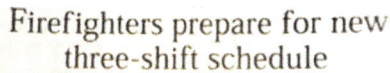

The Leavenworth Fire Department is said to be the first department in the state of Kansas.

It was established in 1855. I believe that designation gives the firefighters a sense of pride. The firefighters are well dressed and hung on to their identification strongly.

For example, I mentioned to one of the Battalion Chiefs that their arm patch looked more like a law enforcement patch and that it was kind of an old school generic looking thing. That Battalion Chief shot back a message that the men would sharply oppose changing it. Hence, I didn't propose changing it again.

I found that the equipment wasn't new, but it wasn't old either. And it was well taken care of. The department operates out of 3 fire stations, one that was poorly built and positioned poorly and the other two stations super special, especially Station 1 Headquarters.

The department operates under a 2-shift system which is highly dysfunctional. Most people, including myself, have a hard time even understanding it.

Standard operational procedures are lacking in updates, and there were simply none for medical response. Some changes needed to be made immediately, while others could take time.

Now, on to the stories.

VS. 3 SHIFT SYSTEM

I met first with my 2 Assistant Chiefs, then all the department members immediately after my arrival. This was a directive given to me in a book

There"s a book I recently read called – In Your First 100 Days.

My 2 Assistant Chiefs and I wrote a report in the first two weeks that identified the conditions of the department including the changes that needed to be made immediately. One of those changes needed immediately was a change from their 2-shift system to a 3- shift system.

After the report the City Commissioners gave us the green light to go forward with the change. The shift system change required a complete set of new officers, mechanics, and drivers. Within the first 90 days we conducted promotional exams and then badge pinning ceremonies.

A GREAT ASSISTANT CHIEF

He is a man of small stature, but one must not be fooled into judging one by size. Mark Demaranville was one of my Assistant Chiefs during my time in Leavenworth.

He made his mark with me right away when we decided to pursue a change from the department's dysfunctional 2-shift operational system, to a 3-shift system used by all other departments.

My understanding of the 2-shift system was poor, so I decided to have him explain it in our report to the Commissioners. His report was a work of art. I have no doubt that Mark helped the Commissioners understand the system too and it had an impact on their decision to vote in favor of our request to make the change.

I'm proud of our report and still have a copy of it today.

I suggested some things for Mark to get in preparation for him to take the Leavenworth Fire Department's fire chief's position upon my departure. Sharing with him that my stay in Leavenworth would be short. He checked off every single one of the items.

Mark's conversations with the public were a "work of art." I swear the man could teach public speaking at the collegiate level.

Another area where Mark was remarkable was his "lack of credit need" for accomplishments. He didn't need to be praised. Many times, he would put Administrative Staff as the author when it was totally him.

I was thrilled when Mark got the Leavenworth Fire Chief's position upon my departure. A well-deserved decision.

I appreciate everything he did for me. I was one lucky man to have him on my administrative staff.

PARTNERSHIPS

One of the first things I identified immediately upon my arrival as fire chief was the lack of partnerships.

Number one on the list was the ambulance service.

The fire department had only been running medical calls for a short time, but I heard the chief before me make it known that he was going to take over the ambulance service.

This made him about as popular as the ugly grade school kid.

Ambulance Director Jamie Miller wasn't going to give him one ounce of support. And support was needed badly.

My fire department had no protocols, no medical director, and no training program.

After I was able to convince Jamie that I absolutely had no plan for taking over his operation, he was a mountain of help. He let us use his protocols and he got their medical director to serve as our medical director – at no cost. He also let us use his training classes in return for using our state-of-the-art training room at headquarters.

The next partnership developed was between our department and the Fort Leavenworth fire department. The agreement was one that called for each department to assist the other upon request by radio.

The Fort Leavenworth Command School offered to provide us with leadership training. The Command school provides training to the United States upper-level Generals. And is considered the most elite leadership training available.

A GOOD BATTALION CHIEF

I had the pleasure of visiting Leavenworth Battalion Chief Mark Baustian last week about his career and his upcoming retirement. He shared some stories about memorable fires, his favorite song (Stormy Monday), his favorite movie (Forest Gump), and the story of how he acquired a nickname.

Forest Gump? — Interesting.

Mark told me that on his first day on the fire department he met with Fire Chief Patzwald. The Chief asked Mark, "Boy, what's your sole purpose in this fire department?"

To which Mark answered – "To do whatever you tell me Chief!"

The Chief barked back at Mark, "Damnit, Baustian! You're a damn genius! That is the most outstanding answer I have ever heard. You must have an IQ of 160. You are gifted, Baustian."

For some reason, Mark fit in at the FD like one of them round pegs. Mark explained, "It's not hard. You just make your bed real neat and remember to stand up straight and always answer every question with "Yes, Sir."

Then Mark recalled the first meeting with his Captain – Captain Ed Jordan. Captain Jordan checked out his fire gear, including his boots. He stressed to Mark that these were "Magic Boots – and they could take him anywhere." He also told Mark that, "Fire is like a box of chocolates. You never know what you're going to get."

Those words of wisdom no more than left Captain Jordan's lips then the alarm sounded. It was a working fire on his first day. Mark was riding on the back of the engine, hanging on for dear life with Driver Jim Spencer driving like a Bat out of Hades when they hit the railroad tracks – Mark's magic boots lifted him off the tailboard, tossing him 3 feet high into the air. Good thing those boots were magic!

It was like this throughout Mark's career. On his first day as a relief driver, he "laid out" the engine. It seemed like Mark and Fire went together like peas and carrots.

But that doesn't mean Mark didn't have a few close calls. One close call involved another firefighter – Johnny Johnston JJ. JJ was a senior firefighter with a bit of a hearing problem – especially when he didn't wear his hearing aids. And that was the case one cold, "Stormy Monday" night.

JJ was inside fighting the structure fire when everyone was told to "Get Out!" The problem is you can't follow an order that you didn't hear. Mark had to make an entry into the structure to deliver the message. He tapped JJ on his back and gave him the emergency message – "Run JJ Run!"

Moments after they were safely out – the roof dropped like a pancake on the area they had just left.

Mark was always in the limelight. He recalled the time the fire department staged a photo opportunity with the Leavenworth Times. Mark rappelled from the department's 102' aerial basket. Before leaving, the reporter asked for the name of the person rappelling. Somehow, he misheard the answer to his question and the front-page cover story identified the Rappeller as "Mark Mustang."

Mark's momma was livid and wanted the newspaper to do a retraction. They wouldn't. Mark told his momma to let it go, adding, "Stupid is as stupid does."

Mark concluded their conversation by saying, "You can tell a lot about a person by their shoes, where they go, where they've been." He added; "I've worn lots of shoes. I bet if I think about it real hard I can remember my first pair of shoes."

Asked what he would miss most about the fire department Mark said, "The Guys." Firefighters don't get all mushy, but it seemed like Mark was saying, "I just wanted to tell you guys, I Love You." And, if not for that same firefighter trait, I'm sure they would say right back, "We love you too, Mark."

And that's all I have to say about that.

P.S. On a serious note – I was blessed to have had Mark Baustian serving as a Battalion Chief during my time as Fire Chief for the City of Leavenworth. I know the others who worked with him feel equally blessed. Congratulations on a great career!

LFD FIRE SAFETY MESSAGE

Chief Moody congratulates the Leavenworth Fire Department first coloring contest.

First, second, and third place winners were for grades kindergarten through fifth grade.

A first-place winner was selected for a special needs category. Organized by Executive Assistant Cary Collins.

THANK YOU FOR THE BLESSINGS

Kansas emergency service lost a superstar in years' past by the name Bill Brubaker. Anybody who's anybody in Kansas emergency service knew Bill. He was a Chief Officer with the City of Lawrence before retiring to take a position as a Regional Emergency Manager with the State of Kansas. A fellow emergency manager recently posted a request for folks to post one word that described Bill – a way to recognize and thank him. I suppose that request was prompted by the upcoming Christmas. I would like to take that a step further.

Christmas is many things to many people. Most recognize the day with gifts, family time, and thanks for the blessings. I would like to address that last one – specifically the blessings of working with emergency service providers in Kansas, past and present.

Thank you for your selflessness. You could've used your talent in a field that would've brought you more self-wealth, but instead you chose this one – one that has brought wellbeing to others including myself. You made sure that I went home at the end of my shift.

Thank you for your bravery. Trench cave-ins, swift waters, vehicle accidents, grain elevator falls, floods, tornados, hurricanes, fires, and hazmat spills. For one to say they never experienced fear is being dishonest or plain stupid. The basic framework of bravery is intrinsic, but the depth of the quality is learned. Everyone needs a role model. Your bravery developed and reinforced my bravery.

Thank you for the courage. It's a close cousin to bravery, but one that crosses over to other areas. You stood up for what was right even when it wasn't a popular stand. At times your actions may have even hurt your career. When I think of your courage, I gently shake my head with amazement and smile.

Thank you for the inspiration. You taught me that just about anything could be done. You showed me what it looked like and what it felt like to perform a lifesaving feat. You kept going when it hurt – both physically and mentally. You made me want to be like you.

Thank you for the love. Love isn't something most emergency workers discuss. It isn't easy to define, but there's nothing more important. You can't do what we do in emergency service without caring a lot, without loving those you do it with. I love you all – past and present.

LFD & FORT LEAVENWORTH

The Leavenworth Fire Department devotes a lot of effort to train entry level Firefighters. But in the past, there hasn't been much leadership training for the department officers.

I told the press that firefighters pick up a lot by watching other supervisors. But leadership development is something that should be formally addressed.

Assistant Chief Mark Demaranville said, "It will improve our current officers and prepare our future officers."

We are having the Army Management Staff College at Fort Leavenworth help us with the training. A plan has been put together for the program and it includes things such as developing values for the LFD as well as purpose, vision, and mission statement.

UNDER PRESSURE

Each part of the experience is different.

You drive by the crumpled vehicles in the median, steam rising from the still warm engines, broken parts on the pavement crunch beneath your vehicle's tires. You envision trauma, possibly even death. But do you ever wonder what it's like to be the rescue team?

Looking at a picture or driving by an accident scene is much different than working an accident. It's akin to the difference between losing a loved one and being a consoling friend, or like watching a YouTube video of a young kid being beaten by a group of thugs, versus being the beaten kid.

For starters, what you see is but a fraction of what the rescuer sees. The obvious is that you don't see the patient – the blood in all its red versions, pale yellow marble-looking fatty tissue, protruding bones, and body parts encased by metal like shrink wrap plastic.

Then there are the non-patient sights. The personal bible crumpled in the back seat, an empty child car-seat, a single partially unlaced boot lying on the shoulder of the roadway.

Only the rescue team will sense the smell and taste. The scene's odor flows in through your nostrils down to the back palate striking the taste buds near the base of the tongue. You sense the sweet taste of antifreeze, the homeless person odor of diesel fuel, the rotten egg smell of battery acid, and soon the smell of your own perspiration.

As you drive by you might experience some sound – the buzz of the rescue tools. But you won't hear the change of the engine as it strains from a difficult cut. You won't hear the sound of twisting, cutting metal. You won't take in the short necessary messages between rescuers. Nor will you hear the words of impending doom spoken from a soul about to leave this life.

Touch is another sense that only the rescuer experiences. Popping bubble wrap is the feel of air pockets beneath the skin caused by a punctured lung. The twisting pressure of the Jaws tool pulls sideways on your grip, your hands slick with the slime of diesel fuel and motor oil.

And, most profoundly you won't sense the pressure. Maybe you think you understand the pressure because you were an athlete back in high school or you have had to meet a short deadline with a project at work. But no life lies in the balance of a basketball or a football game or a missed deadline. The outcome is hurt feelings, not loss of life.

Saving a life is the goal of the rescue team, but the clock is ticking.

Will they get the patient rescued in time? The right rescue cuts in the right spots equal many minutes difference. Ticktock, ticktock. Will the medics deliver the proper care in time? Spending too much time can be the minutes the surgeon needed. Ticktock, ticktock. Did you park the trucks correctly to protect the scene, did you disconnect the battery, so a spark doesn't ignite the standing fuel? Skipping steps that require extra time can kill too. Ticktock, ticktock.

And what pay do these heroes get for this life saving work they do? Surely it mirrors the salaries of those who play games. Ironically, it's the opposite – many do it for no pay, and the others do it for a modest sum. Rescue workers provide their life-saving service for the right reasons.

So, here's the point of this story.

You'll never fully understand what a rescuer goes through, but that doesn't mean you can't appreciate what they do. There's a famous song by the group Queen called "Under Pressure." When you hear that song in the future, stop and think about rescuers and what they do.

And when you see one, tell them "Thank You."

THE GREATEST SALESMAN

The inscription inside the front cover of the little red book read, "Christmas 1977" – Steve – *We decided to give you this tremendous book as you will begin to see how it can influence your life – Our Love, Aunt Lizzie & Uncle Lloyd."* The book was titled, "The Greatest Salesman in the World."

"The Greatest Salesman in the World" is a story about a young camel tender named Hafid who is given a gift of ten scrolls, each scroll with a secret to success. The beauty of the story – as author Og Mandino knew – was the secrets can be applied to any career or just life in general.

This past week fourteen Stafford County students began the journey to become an Emergency Medical Technician EMT. So, I thought, "What better idea than to examine how Og Mandino's secrets could help ensure the success of an EMT student."

THE POWER OF GOOD HABITS

Good habits to an EMT can be the difference between life and death, both for the patient and for the EMT.

Replace your equipment and supplies after each usage – practice your skills and study your protocols. Wear your gloves, ensure the scene is safe before entering, and take command of the scene.

LIVE EACH DAY AS IF IT WERE YOUR LAST – GREET EACH DAY WITH LOVE IN YOUR HEART

Mandino listed these as two separate secrets. I combined them because it seems impossible to have one without the other.

A few years 'back emergency crews worked a fatality accident. The gentleman who lost his life left a wife and four young children. Emergency workers are taught the lesson of living each day as it if were your last way too many times. It shouldn't take more than once.

Once you've learned the reality of how quickly life can end, greeting each day with love in your heart only seems natural.

YOU ARE NATURES GREATEST MIRACLE

An EMT is given a peek into the world of the rich as well as that of the poor. It gives you a unique perspective. Some people's homes are filled with gold, others with tin. To the holder, tin is as valuable as gold.

All people are nature's greatest miracle. You'll learn that lesson after a few road trips with each.

MASTER YOUR EMOTIONS

Few jobs will invoke stronger emotional response, both with you and the customer. People that are sick or injured have a flood of emotions that are only superseded by those of their loved ones.

Success or failure – life or death – might depend upon how well "you" master your emotions.

THE POWER OF LAUGHTER

Emergency workers learn this secret quickly and practice it often. I would only add a small bit of advice. Laughter can be a powerful secret to success, but it must be used in the right place at the right time. The family or public will not understand. Keep smiles and laughter out of sight of the public during an emergency.

MULTIPLY YOUR VALUE EVERY DAY – ALL IS WORTHLESS WITHOUT ACTION

Here's another two secrets that seem to go together. Multiplying your value every day doesn't mean you must strive to attain a promotion or advancement, although that isn't a bad thing. What it means is you should strive to be the best you can be at what you do. Read, listen, watch – you'll be amazed at what you learn.

And remember that talking about doing something isn't doing it. Likewise, talking about what somebody else needs to do is usually of absolutely no value.

PRAY TO GOD FOR GUIDANCE

This last secret needs a little clarification. I don't believe the words were intended to be taken literally. You probably aren't going to get an email from the Big Guy, no matter how much you pray. So, maybe a better choice of words for this secret would be, "Do what God would want."

I personally think God would want us to – "Follow the nine secrets."

JUST THE GOOD TIMES

The call location was an address in one of the most expensive neighborhoods in town. The patient was a middle-aged man that was depressed about some things, and it just got to be too much. An overdose would end it all. And it did.

That was an emergency call that took place during my early career many years ago. Over three decades in emergency service hasn't helped me understand many of the tragedies we

face. But it has given me a unique perspective on how emergency responders deal with tragedy.

One of the toughest medics I ever worked with was a woman. Most thought she was a rough, tough broad that had a heart of steel. They were wrong. More than once I saw the tears she tried to hide. But she was tough – tough enough to work a complete career.

Some believe medics are wired with a shortage of compassion. And that might be true for a few, but it's not the norm. Here's what I think.

I believe most medics metaphorically put on a full set of body armor when they respond to emergencies. The incident – as we call it – is focused on the patient. If the patient happens to be deceased, then we transform the situation into a learning experience.

That explains the incident itself, but what about the large amount

of time after the call? Does the body armor stay on indefinitely? I don't believe it does. This is what I believe is the second piece to the puzzle.

It's a concept called, "Just the Good Times." An episode in the sitcom called "Everybody Loves Raymond" explains it well.

The lead character in the sitcom is named Raymond. As the best man in his brother's wedding, he gives a toast. About everything bad that could happen with family interference had just happened. But Raymond's message to the family and friends was that they weren't going to focus on those times. They would only remember the good times.

That I believe is what medics do in their professional life. Unfortunately, I also believe they do it subconsciously. I say unfortunately, because medics typically aren't any better than the average Joe at blocking out bad events in their everyday lives.

I challenge all medics to recognize what a great skill you have. But take it a step further and practice it in your everyday life. And help other non-medics do the same.

Just the good times, just the good times.

Dedicated to Paramedic Jane Steen.

HAPPINESS IS A CHOICE

My son recently sent me a link to an article written by a Portuguese photographer. The photographer traveled to a garbage dump in Africa where upwards of 700 people live. These people forage amongst the waste for food and recyclables. Words can't describe the human suffering depicted in the photos.

Yet, what struck the photographer most was, "Despite all the circumstances of how they live, they keep on showing their kindness and happiness and hospitality" he said. Emergency responders don't see happiness anything remotely like that garbage dump in Africa, but we are in the "worst day of your life" business. And, yet it doesn't appear to me we're any less happy than the population at large. Why is that?

Here's my theory.

I believe happiness is a choice. And yes, happiness might be an easier choice given favorable circumstances, yet it's still a choice.

I compare it to Mr. Potato Head. You can dress Mr. Potato Head however you choose and give him whatever expression you choose. And the smile is no different coupled with the fanciest ensemble versus the most modest.

This realization might be what depresses many who work their entire lives with the goal of wealth. Once wealth is attained it doesn't guarantee

There's a song recorded by Bobby McFerrin called "Don't Worry, Be Happy." The ending goes like this: *"Put a smile on your face – Don't bring everybody down like this – Don't worry, it will soon pass – Whatever it is – Don't worry, be happy."*

If you don't think every day is a great day, schedule a ride-along with your local ambulance service. You may see someone that's not going to have another day. That might be what brings it into perspective for those at the garbage dump.

PERFECT PROPOSAL

Last evening, I witnessed the perfect proposal – a marriage proposal by my son Matthew to his future bride Erin. And, today as I listened to fire experts explain another perfect proposal – a prescribed burn proposal –

I thought about the commonality between the two proposals.

Both start with preparation. The fire side involves meeting the fire chief, getting his blessing, and making sure he will "yes." A well-detailed plan ensures the proposal will have every chance of being a success. On the marriage side the preparation begins with meeting the future in-laws, getting their blessing, and making sure the chosen one will say "yes." With this being one of the most important moments in your life, it's also vital that every detail be planned.

The next step after getting the green light is pre-planning the site location. For fire this requires determining the make-up of the burn product and the needed wind direction on the day of the fire. Now, flip over to the marriage proposal pre-planned site location. My son chose Salina's historic Stiefel Theater stage as the site location. Both sets of parents were pre-positioned ahead of time, alongside the stage, and out of Erin's direct line of sight.

Equipment is the next piece to the puzzle. The fire list is a bit longer than the marriage list. Trucks, water, ATVs, swatters, and drip torches are just a few items on the list. The controlled burner must follow any local or state requirements. The marriage proposal equipment is vitally important, but simpler – the "ring."

At last, comes the time everyone's waited for – the moment to shine. The prescribed burner makes sure the weather conditions meet the pre-plan, equipment is in place, and the call is made to the dispatcher. The prescribed burn proposal is perfect. So, how did the marriage proposal go?

My son walked Erin onto the stage facing away from us parents. She seemed a bit perturbed they had taken this sidestep from the restaurant trip he had told her they were headed for. Then he turned her around towards the open theater and to us. There was a look of shock and wonderment. Then, the drop to the knee and moments later the perfect marriage proposal was complete.

It's funny how a perfect proposal is a perfect proposal.

EFFICIENT LEARNING ON A BUDGET

This past week the annual Kansas Emergency Manager's cadre meeting – along with Advanced Presentations, Briefings, and Facilitation Methodology – took place in Topeka. During the cadre meeting there was a brainstorming session. In that session I brought up the idea of utilizing technology to eliminate travel for the many meetings we emergency managers attend. My suggestion was met with astounding opposition from one participant – *"It won't work, we must meet face-to-face."*

Being one that dislikes absolute statements, I voiced that sentiment back to the opposing party – *"I don't believe you can make a blanket statement about the use of technology."* The conversation didn't go much further than those two briefs, tart comments. But I didn't forget.

The cadre meeting ended. And the next two days were spent on Advanced Presentations, Briefings, and Facilitation Methodology. The finale to that portion of the training was a short presentation from each of the class participants. Remember about my not forgetting? My presentation was titled, "Efficient Learning – Learning on a Budget."

The presentation began with a story about my two sons and baseball. Both of my sons played baseball at an early age. I'm a believer that if you're going to do something, you do it the best you can. So, I found a baseball camp to send my boys to when they were very young. Unfortunately, I found out the primary focus of the camps was to make money for the camp organizer. So, I looked for other options. Being a man of little money, I had to look at low budget options. VHS tapes were the craze back in those days. I found that leaders in baseball had video tapes – and books. I bought both. And the   sons went on to be successful collegiate baseball players.

From baseball we moved to meetings – and back to the philosophy, *"If you're going to do something, you do it the best you can."* I posed the question, *"Is it cost efficient to have 10-20 people drive three hours, spend two hours in a meeting, and then drive three hours to get home?"* You can access numerous websites that have calculators for figuring the cost of a typical meeting. I showed one. And, then I posed the question – *"Is there a more cost-efficient method?"*

That's when I pulled out my Ipad. Double-click on the Facetime icon. And, then a double click on moody47@gmail.com. Within seconds Matthew Moody – my son – appeared on the screen. I walked the

Ipad around the room and introduced Matthew to the instructor and the students.

Matthew was at work in Salina where he takes care of a radio station's websites. After the introductions, Matthew gave the class an overview of how Facetime works. He then explained a new meeting product that Google is putting out. That product will allow bigger groups, from various locations, to meet. All the participant's pictures/video will be shown along the bottom of the screen. The person from the group who's speaking the loudest will be portrayed as a large picture/video on the screen.

What's the cost of Facetime and Google? Zero. Gas costs? Zero. Food costs? Zero. Motel costs? Zero. I finished my short presentation by stating the obvious, *"Americans will be required to do more with less in the future."* Because, as we all know, Uncle Sam is stone broke.

The sad part is it shouldn't have taken a crisis to do better – us or the federal government.

THE GREAT WOMAN THEORY

Two of the departments I worked in had Executive Assistants – Judy Piercy in Salina and Cary Collins in Leavenworth. As already talked about in this book was The Great Man Theory. It needs to be looked at with these two Great Women.

Judy and Cary are support personnel that make them Heroes as much as does the emergency personnel.

I must be getting old. I say that because I often find myself reflecting in time. Those scenes that come to life are ones that involve people – sometimes great people. I would like to tell you about two that fit that title.

Wikipedia explains *"The Great Man theory is a 19th-century idea according to which history can be largely explained by the impact of "great women", or heroes: highly influential individuals who, due to either their personal charisma, intelligence, wisdom, or political skill utilized.*

The Great Woman Theory has been studied and explained by scholars, but I don't think you need to be a scholar to spot the Great Ones. The two I worked with were Judy Piercy and Cary Collins. Collins.

I have met some great people in my sixty-six years of life, but none better than Judy and Cary.

These two always made sure the firefighters got paid and they helped with the many reports that supported the organization.

I was a lucky man because I would say these two were the best that I had the fortune of working who fit The Great Woman Theory.

LITTLE BOY NAMED CHRISTIAN

The call came into dispatch early one Sunday evening. It was a young mother, frantic because her young son had set a fire in his bedroom.

Dispatch called me because fire crews were out on other emergencies. And the need wasn't to extinguish the fire – mom had already done that – it was to do something with the boy.

The mother met me curbside in front of her small home as the sun was setting. She explained that her husband was incarcerated, she had two young sons, and the older one – Christian – had recently grown fascinated with cigarette lighters. Today's fire was his second.

She went right to the point of her call and asked, "What can you do?"

I politely told the mother this was a problem more suitable for somebody in mental health, not a fire chief. She explained that Christian had already talked to one of those folks and it hadn't helped. I could feel the helplessness from the crackle of her voice and the watery look in her eyes.

I told the mother I would visit with Christian if she called the mental health professionals too. I gave Christian as stern a talking to as I ever have a young child. I raised my voice to just under a shout, berating him for thinking so little of his younger brother and mother. Finally, I told him I was through for now, but I wasn't through – I was coming back tomorrow.

I then turned to the mother and told her to search every single inch of the house for lighters and that I would come back the next day.

As I drove towards home, I thought about what to do, knowing fear seldom invokes long term change. The answer came to me like a message from above. I would call on the young boy's sense of responsibility, his manhood.

The next day I purchased a gift card with a fire department theme and placed inside a St. Florian medallion – The Patron Saint of Firefighters. I explained with my writing the significance of the medallion, what it means to firefighters, and the responsibility Christian would have as a carrier – to remember me and the agreements we had.

Christian and his mother were standing in the yard when I arrived the next day. Lying on the ground was close to forty novelty lighters, stolen from neighborhood stores. I locked eyes with Christian and could sense his fear. I directed him to come with me to the fire car. He started to get in the back seat, and I redirected him to the front.

I again locked eyes with Christian, but fear was no longer my motive. I talked to Christian not as a boy, but as a young man. I explained to Christian that I could tell that he was intelligent and had so much potential in his life. But I also explained that he needed to be the man of the home. I told him that I hoped someday he would consider becoming a firefighter. Afterwards, we got out of the car, shook hands, and we parted. I thought that would probably be the last I would hear of Christian. It wasn't.

Several months later a friend of Christian's family stopped me at the courthouse, asked if I was Chief Moody, and handed me an envelope. Inside was a letter with two medals taped to it and a message from Christian.

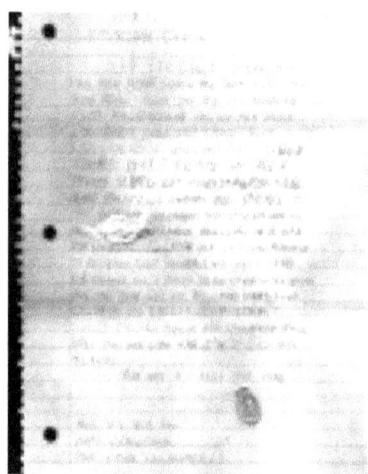

Dear Mr. Cheif,

Hi Fire Cheif Steve,

How have you bean sence the last time you seen me. Thank you for the meatle you sent me and thank you for the card. I've been good and I haven't bean lighting fires and hiding lighters and knifes. Thank you for your time and the card I truley appreciate everything you have done you are an awesome guy. I love you fore your help and the charm – here's one fore you as well. {Medallion taped here} Please take care of it and remember me every time you look at it. I have potential to do the right thaing. I will start to do for others as I want to be treated.

You went out of your way for me. I hope that we can count on you when I have a problem.

Thanks, again for evrething please call me any time and I will call you as well.

You are a hero my hero. {Medallion taped here}

Here's my last one fore extra luck. Your friend Christian.

I have never forgotten you Christian – and have always cherished both your letter, and the medallions.

FIREFIGHTERS, MEDICS PRAISED FOR RESCUE

They met as Misti Gartz and her two children were rescued from a second story window while a fire raged in the Leavenworth woman's apartment.

But Gartz and her children had a chance to see their rescuers under better circumstances when they visited the Leavenworth Fire Department,

They were present for a ceremony that recognized the firefighters as well as the Leavenworth EMS medics who provided care for the family.

I presented certificates to the firefighters and EMS personnel who responded to the call that day.

I also presented a toy firefighter dressed in turnout gear. Firefighters took turns signing the packaging for the toy.

LEADERSHIP PARTICIPANT PROJECT

About 15 people, including myself, were in the year's Leadership Leavenworth-Lansing class.

The goal of the program is to establish a network of community leaders and provide upcoming leaders with an opportunity to grow and develop with help from people in leadership positions.

The students chose as their class project the installation of smoke/carbon monoxide detectors. The detectors were donated by Lowe's home-improvement business.

The detectors were installed by the Leadership class.

THE LEAVENWORTH ENDING

I was happy with Leavenworth and loved the firefighters, but in 2009 I decided I wanted a change of pace.

LFD NEWSLETTER

It was popular in Salina, and it was just as popular in Leavenworth.

The Fire Department Newsletter.

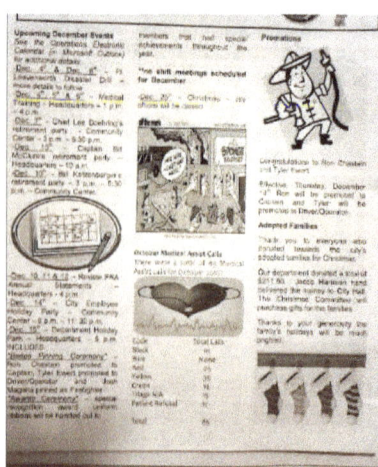

But there were differences between the two. Executive Assistant Cary Collins took on the job of writing the publishment and she had many new ideas for additional features.

Birthdays and any special things happening at the department or with a firefighter. A special trivia section was another feature.

The newsletter made it easy to write the annual report.

LFD HALLOWEEN FIRE SAFETY

It was the brainchild of SFD public educator Deb Weaver and husband Bill.

The SFD Halloween Fire Safety House was put on for several years and then it was discontinued for reasons that I don't know.

I thought it would be a great fit for Leavenworth, so I asked the Salina Fire Chief if we could use it. He said "yes."

There will be some changes though. Instead of having it at one of the fire stations, we would have it in the city's gymnasium. The gymnasium had side access that would work great for entering and exiting.

Next, we decided that we needed a couple of additional rooms. I reached out to the State Prison Warden for help. He said he was happy

to have several inmate artists build and paint the rooms at no expense other than the supplies.

Salina used both drama students and firefighters as the role players in the rooms. I reached out to the high school drama class teacher. He said his class would fill all the needs for actors.

Good friends SFD Public Educator Deb Weaver and SFD Training Chief Willis Sutton made the drive to Leavenworth for both days.

They did this just to help with whatever might be needed.

The event was a huge success. Letters of thanks and praise were received from many.

The show was put on again the next year.

CHAPTER 4
MY CAREER IN STAFFORD COUNTY

THE BEGINNING

I still loved being a fire chief, so I took a job with Stafford County KS as the emergency service director, overseeing ambulance operations, fire operations, and emergency management operations.

But, my time in Stafford County began two weeks before my paid start.

Stafford County Firefighter Dennis Simmons suffered a fatal heart attack when returning to the fire station after a grassland fire.

I would make two round trips to Stafford County from Leavenworth.

The first trip was to meet and console the family. And to make sure all the necessary information was put together to receive federal life insurance benefits.

The second trip was to attend the funeral, meet the firefighters and give a heart-felt speech.

Most Stafford emergency responders are volunteers, and this brought me a new-found respect for those who do their emergency job without pay.

BOX TURTLE TIM

One of the great things about living in a rural community is the wildlife. I'm served a variety of different animal sightings on my commute to work – sometimes it's a graceful white-tail deer, other times it's a red fox, or lately a colorful peacock. This day it was a turtle.

The little box turtle was standing squarely in the middle of the road as I drove past him. Then, I stopped.

Lately, I'd seen several animals lying dead on the roadway – struck by vehicles. I didn't want this turtle to have the same fate. He must be moved.

But I thought how my grandson would love to see this little fellow – he was coming to visit tomorrow – as I got out of my truck and walked towards the turtle. I don't know how right it was, but I decided.

I decided "Tim the Turtle" would visit the Moody House at Pooh Corner in Stafford – for a day.

I placed him in a big box with leaves, grapes, and orange skins for snacks. Early the next day grandson Macoy arrived. We spent the morning with Tim watching him walk around in our front yard.

But I explained to Macoy that Tim was a wild creature and needed to return to the wild. Early the next morning we took Tim back to the country and released him in a safe spot.

I did Tim a favor by moving him from the roadway, but he did me an even bigger favor – he brought joy to my grandson for a day.

Thanks Tim.

TERRY SPRADLEY – ONE OF THE TEAM

I loved building partnerships. And I always looked at the press to build one with them too.

Stafford County had a man that carried all the roles of a newspaper man – writing, photography, and publishing. Just like the emergency responders, he covered the entire county.

I established a friendship with Terry and made him a part of the team. I outfitted him with a safety vest and a radio.

He was an incredible man that unfortunately died shortly after I left Stafford County.

MEDIC 4 MIRACLE

The dispatcher sent out a very special message – *"Medic 4 – you need to respond to the 100 block of Newell Street for a woman in labor having strong contractions."*

Medic 4 arrived on-scene in short order and found exactly what the dispatcher had said, a young lady in active labor. And this wasn't her first child. And one last detail – she wanted to **PUSH!**

Our message to our patient was short – **DON'T!**

Heather followed our simple advice, but somebody else factored into the equation once we got in the ambulance. Baby decided she wasn't waiting any longer and out came **"Medic 4 Miracle."**

One year later – we gathered to celebrate Eva's first birthday. Eva was given a fitting ride to her 1st birthday party – in the back of (yes you guessed it) Medic 4.

Heather had another surprise for Eva – the COOLEST cake ever – it was a Medic 4 replica!

In addition to the Medic 4 cake – Eva got her very own little cake. After about an hour little Eva had enough frosting smeared over her that it brought back visions of what she looked like one year ago.

Medic 4 Miracle – thanks for inviting us to your celebration.

CHRISTMAS TRIP CUT SHORT

I was given permission by a patient and his wife to tell their story about a Christmas trip cut short. It's a story about a cute little couple from New Orleans that started out on a train trip to Los Angeles, but ended up in Stafford, Kansas.

Samuel and Shirley were taking a train trip to visit a sister – a long, long train trip. It started in New Orleans and would end in Los Angeles on Christmas Eve. But it wasn't to be.

Shirley thinks it could've been the constant clack, clack, clack of the railroad tracks. Samuel mentioned it as they were rolling through the Chicago area. But Shirley thought sleep would make things better. It didn't.

She awakened the next morning and Samuel was now more than ever not himself. Nothing he was saying made much sense. So, Shirley alerted train officials.

The train had just passed a station in Hutchinson, Kansas. They decided the next stop would be too far. If they could get a medical team to meet them, they would stop at the very next town – a little Kansas town called Stafford, population one thousand.

The dispatcher informed the train representative that an ambulance crew could meet them. They would meet on Main Street on the north edge of

town, yards away from the long-ago closed train station. The dispatcher paged out the medical team – a volunteer crew.

The ambulance pulled up perpendicular to the tracks with the headlights shining through the light snow towards the faintly visible abandoned Stafford train station. Seconds later the first sign of the approaching train arrived – the bellowing blast of a horn. The conductor kept the blare going until the train itself arrived.

The engine passed the ambulance and continued onward for what seemed like about seven cars. Then, it came to an easy stop. How the conductor stopped the right car with its doorway at the right point is a mystery.

A Porter in full dress with cap stepped through the opened door and gently placed a step stool on the cold snow-packed pavement. The medics found Samuel and Shirley standing right inside the doorway.

Samuel wasn't much aware of what was going on, but because of his condition he wasn't interested in interacting with the medical team. With a little determination the team was still able to coax him onto their cot, but treatment was another story.

A blood pressure cuff and some limb-placed electrodes. That was the extent of allowed treatment. But that would be enough to identify the problem. The blood pressure was too high, way too high.

It was a short trip to the hospital on the other end of town – one mile straight south and a couple blocks to the east. The physician assistant came from his home but was there about as quickly as the train had arrived.

Samuel received immediate treatment to lower his blood pressure, but he would need to be admitted. Later that day they discovered the stay would need to be longer. A total of 72 hours in the hospital is the Medicare requirement. December 23rd plus two additional days = December 25th = Christmas Day.

This could've been a problem for Shirley because there's no motel in Stafford. But rural caregivers know how to care for people, even if they don't have all the big city equipment. Samuel and Shirley were given a room for two.

The question now was, "How to get home?" Because of Samuel's medical condition the doctor ruled out the train. An airplane was the choice. All that was needed was an early Christmas morning ride – a one-hundred-mile trip to Wichita, Kansas. My wife and I came to the rescue.

Rosie made the arrangements and early Christmas morning Samuel and Shirley took a ride to Wichita. They arrived home in New Orleans in time for dinner with their children. It was a Christmas trip cut short, but one that will surely be a Christmas to remember.

FOLLOW-UP

Just the other day news came from Samuel and Shirley. The couple sent a heart-felt "Thank You" card along with a New Orleans food care package. Here's what the card said –

"*We will never forget the kindness and love and sacrifice that you showed us in our time of need. May God continue to bless all of you and your families. You will always be in our prayers. We will always love you.*

Unfortunately, at the end of the "Thank You" card Shirley also shared some sad news.

"P.S.: My sister passed on December 31st and we went to Los Angeles for the services. We've been back home for about a week."

Samuel and Shirley – *"We will always love you too!"*

ONE SICK INDIAN

He was traveling to America with the goal of earning money to send back to his family in India. The young man would do computer work in Kansas City, but first he was traveling to Chicago – by train – to meet a friend of the family. The traveler's name was Rashid.

The train ride started in Los Angeles, and everything went well until one o'clock Monday morning when they reached the Kansas mid-point. Rashid wasn't feeling well. He had a dry cough, a low-grade fever, and lips that looked like the flaking bark of a sycamore tree.

For some reason the train's medic diagnosed Rashid's condition as serious and ordered his immediate removal from the train. Up ahead was the little town of St. John with a train station that was long ago closed. This was where they would stop. Ambulance medics Misty and

Lori gave Rashid a short ambulance ride to Stafford County Hospital where the doctor diagnosed a simple virus.

Afterwards, Rashid walked across the street to the town's only hotel without knowing how he would get to Chicago. There are no buses in Stafford County. There are no taxis in Stafford County. And the train only does drop offs in Stafford County, no pick-ups. But Stafford County cares for people. Rashid was picked up and taken to Chief Moody's home for lunch, then given a ride to the Hutchinson train station.

A little over a year ago another sick train rider and his spouse dropped off the train in Stafford County. They were later given a ride to Wichita to catch a flight home. That one was Christmas Day – this one was simply the anniversary of the signing of the Treaty of Mangalore.

Rural America comes through again.

CHARLES "WILDSEEDER" SAMEK

The body was lying on the shoulder of the highway two miles south of St. John – beside it a dark jumbo trash bag. Naturally, I pulled over to check out the situation.

Just as I was stepping out of my vehicle the body rose from the ground. It was that of a bearded middle-aged man wearing a ball cap. Written on the bill and encircling the upper part of the cap was the word *"SOUL-CRAFT."*

His name was Charles Samek and he was a hitchhiker headed to Vermont. Charles asked if I would give him a

ride to the Highway 50 junction for a dollar. I said, *"I won't give you a ride for a dollar, but I will give you a ride."*

As we talked Charles told me his planned path was through Hutchinson. Since Stafford was my destination, I offered to take him there instead. He accepted the offer.

During the short ride Charles explained that he was Czechoslovakian, a conspiracy theorist, had a master's degree in English, and had been hitchhiking for forty-five years. Charles asked me if I knew anything about Blackwater and the connection with the Boston Bombings. When

I said "no" – he let burst a long cackling laugh.

And then the trip ended. As Charles exited my vehicle with his jumbo bag, I asked him for a photo to use for a story. Charles was happy to do so. As I shook his hand he asked if I would send the story to wildseederus@yahoo.com. He said, "Email it to me and I'll read it on the Internet at my next library stop."

I don't advocate giving rides to hitchhikers, but please don't pass up an opportunity to do something nice for somebody when given the chance. The story of a young man named Zach Sobiech reminded me of this principle.

APPRECIATION FOR THE ROCK

I've worked with a lot of people during my emergency service career. The length of these people's emergency careers has varied. Some worked decades, some years, some months, some weeks, and some days.

And some worked their whole careers for the same organization, while others – including myself – worked for several organizations.

The length and quality of careers seems to be as varied as the ways we choose to recognize them when they leave. That may be why we don't always do a good job with recognition. And that brings me to the point of this article.

Assistant Fire Director T.J. Rockenbach brought his time with Stafford County to a close. He accepted a job offer in his home state of Oklahoma.

T.J. didn't work decades in Stafford County, he isn't a lifelong resident, he didn't rescue a house full of children, and he isn't staying in Stafford County. But there's plenty that he did do.

T.J. loves the fire service as much as anybody I've ever met.

It showed with his enthusiasm to help get a new fire station built in St. John – the first combined City/County station in that city. It showed in his efforts to get the department switched over to electronic reporting. It showed when he coordinated the purchase of gear and equipment through two large federal grants.

As a spin-off from his name, I would describe T.J. as "The Rock" when it comes to his fire service dedication.

THE GREAT MAN THEORY

I must be getting old. I say that because I often find myself reflecting in time. Those scenes that come to life are ones that involve people – sometimes great people. I would like to tell you about one.

Wikipedia explains *"The Great Man theory is a 19th-century idea according to which history can be largely explained by the impact of "great men", or heroes: highly influential individuals who, due to either their personal charisma, intelligence, wisdom, or political skill utilized their power in a way that had a decisive historical impact."* The Great Man theory has been studied and explained by scholars, but I don't think you need to be a scholar to spot the Great Ones.

His name is Leon Dunn.

I have met some great people in my sixty-six years of life, but none better than Leon Dunn. He has all the "Great Man" qualities.

On the business side of the equation, you find a man who is highly successful in multiple business ventures. This is unique because even businesses that seem similar are often very different. To be successful in multiple ones says a lot.

He's a man who gets involved with public matters when it's important. This is unique for a businessman. Often the focus of a successful businessman is solely business – there's just no time left in the day. Leon is a man who will "park the tractor."

Leon is a soft-spoken man who when he speaks says volumes. I have watched him sit back, let others say their piece, and then step up after everyone else. He says just a few words – all of them profound.

Financial success requires conservatism. That conservatism is often at odds with giving back to the community. Some who are successful in business never give back, while others wait to give until death comes knocking on their doorstep. Not Leon.

On any given Sunday afternoon, you could find Leon cleaning up a little community like Hudson, Kansas following a church service where he shared a biblical sermon about giving. Leon walks the talk.

FREDDIE THE FIREFIGHTER

Stafford County Firefighters gathered for their first annual dinner, sharing the year's, reflections, and a few words from Baylee.

The wonderful dinner was prepared by Darrell Bauer – Wheatland Café – and provided as a gesture of appreciation by Farm Bureau. After everyone had stuffed themselves to a point of borderline non-walking capacity, it was time to look back on the year's accomplishments.

Reflections started by recalling the many emergencies that responders dealt with in the past year. It included a tornado, highway accidents, a house fire, a power plant fire, and a dry season that at one point included thirty fires in thirty days.

Some of the accomplishments included a new fire station, a new Emergency Operations Center, a new rescue truck, new rescue tools, a refurbished tender, and a new supervisory vehicle.

The evening concluded with a video of music tied in with pictures. But before that video a short essay titled "Freddie the Firefighter" was recited by Baylee Lauffer.

The essay is an adaptation of an essay written by the late great Red Skelton. Stafford County Firefighters loved it. I'm sure Red did too.

FREDDIE THE FIREFIGHTER

Freddie the Firefighter is a little bit of you, and a little bit of me, a little bit of all us, you know? He's found out what courage means.

He knows the value of time.

He knows that our time can end in a moment. We say we don't have time to do this or that. There's plenty of time. The trick is not to waste what we've been given.

And Freddie knows all these things. And so do you.

He doesn't ask anybody for a big salary, because it would be taken from you.

He doesn't ask for a medal or flowering recognition and he knows one more thing...that the kind things he does today may be forgotten by many tomorrow, but the recipient may cherish them over a lifetime. He's nice to everybody because he was taught that man is made in God's image. He's never met God in

person and the next fella just might be him. I would say that Freddie is a little bit of all of us.

CONTROLLED BURNS

New open burning procedure that offers standby trucks staffed with firefighters for a fee.

Included was a fine for not following guidelines.

The fines would come back to haunt me when we sent a bill to a farmer who was a good friend of a commissioner.

But it was the right then to do. We had numerous requests for wildland fires that were out of control.

Firefighters will be safer because of this new policy because of the reduction in out-of-control fires.

ALASKA VACATION

Rosie and I took one of the few vacations we've taken in our lives.

A trip to Alaska. It was on our "Bucket List." I would highly recommend it.

We had a wonderful time.

TORNADO TOPPLED TREE

The weather snuck into Stafford County quickly, like weather often does in Kansas, A Stafford County family was traveling back from Great Bend when the storm hit.

They pulled into a farmstead driveway immediately adjacent to a monstrous cottonwood tree – tornado crossed.

The giant tree fell directly across the family's vehicle. Firefighters were able to rescue the daughter, but the mother and son were killed instantly.

The father/husband showed up on the scene. I had the most difficult responsibility of giving him the sad news.

PROM READY TRIP
Kinberly is not the real name of this young lady.

High school senior Kimberly was getting herself ready for the big night – High School Prom. She had gotten her make-up on and was making the short trip from Stafford to St. John to get her hair dollied up.

Old 50 highway is used by many, and this was the case for Kimberly today. Old highway 50 has a sharp corner about halfway between the two towns. And a sand gravel road intersects the highway at the curve. That sand drifts up on Old 50 highway.

Many youngsters don't think an accident is going to happen to them. And for that reason, they often don't strap on their seatbelt. Kimberly made that choice today. She was distracted, for some reason, when she got to this curve in the highway. And the car rolled into the dirt field.

Kimberly was unresponsive upon Medic 4's arrival. She was quickly extricated and moved to the ambulance. Medical Director Dr. Farmer heard the call dispatched and responded to the scene, arriving at the same time Kimberly was placed in the ambulance. A primary exam found no pulse and no breathing.

What I remember about this call was Kimberly's bright blue eyes. CPR was initiated and blood seeped into the corners of her beautiful eyes. Her eyes and senseless death are forever seared in my memory. Dr. Farmer stopped CPR.

A PERFECT THANKSGIVING

This was the first time the Thanksgiving feast was being held at Mike and Katy's home. Katy was thrilled, but a little nervous. She told Mike,

"I'll take care of all the food preparation, if you just take care of cooking the turkey."

Mike happily accepted that responsibility because he had just received a turkey fryer for his birthday.

Thanksgiving Day the weather was gorgeous. The house smelled of apple pie, mashed potatoes, creamed corn, and a mixture of other goodies. All of Katy's preparations were right on track and it was nearing time for the family to arrive. By all signs this was looking

like it was going to be a "Perfect Thanksgiving.

And Mike was taking care of his one job. He had gently dropped the turkey into the cooker and slipped back into the den to catch some of the commentary on the upcoming football game. It seemed like he'd only been in the den for a few minutes when he heard a blood-curdling cry. *"The garage is on

fire!"* Katy screamed.

By the time the fire department arrived a big part of the detached garage was on fire, along with the corner of the house. Firefighters quickly extinguished the fire, but all thoughts of this being the "Perfect Thanksgiving" were gone.

No time is a good time, for an accident. The crazy thing is most are easily preventable.

Role-play with a holiday safety check list to keep everyone safe. You be the pilot. Go over all the things to be on the look-out for. Have your family members be the co-pilots.
- Wash hands often. *Check*
- Keep cooking attended. *Check*
- If going to another home, immediately look it over for safety concerns. *Check*
- If you have a food allergy, assure the food is not on the menu. *Check*
- Be careful what you shove in your mouth, so you don't choke. *Check*
- Don't drive tired. *Check*
- Don't drink and then drive. *Check*
- Don't distract the driver. *Check*
- Put out any candles. *Check*

A "Perfect Thanksgiving" must be a safe one.

TWO SPECIAL PEOPLE – JOYCE & GREG

The most wonderful thing about being a medic is the people you get to know. Your job is to care for your patient. But what many medics fail to see is the care the patient gives back to you.

During my time in Stafford County, I took care of two special people. And those people gave me as much care as I ever gave them.

Their names were Joyce and Greg.

Joyce and Greg, both left us in May of 2004 to be with the Lord.

Joyce always had a pleasant kind word regardless of the pain she was enduring. A little lady with a mountain of strength. Joyce went through the loss of her husband Joe. The care she gave back was more than I ever dealt with as a medic.

Greg was a man who lived with diabetes for a great number of years. Most people would've been soured by the hand they were dealt with this disease. Not Greg. You would give Greg an amp of Dextrose to bring him back to consciousness and he would look up at you – then crack a Don Rickles type joke at your expense. Thanks for the memories, Joyce, and Greg – the wonderful care you gave me and others.

Rest in peace my friends.

STAFFORD POLICE CHIEF & EMT DOUG BROWN

The late great Doug Brown was a long time City of Stafford Police Chief and a volunteer EMT on the ambulance.

He dedicated an incredible amount of time juggling both roles.

Doug was another one of those who fit the role of "The Great Man" category.

Unfortunately, Doug had some health issues. We lost him several years after I left Stafford County. I'm sure he is sorely missed.

RIBBON CUTTING CEREMONY

Chiefs Mike & Marshal Sanders Cut the Ribbon (Photo Spradley)

The City of St. John and Stafford County had a formal open house and ribbon cutting ceremony to formally open the new combined City/County fire station. This project was the culmination of a lot of work in planning, presentations, and then the actual work itself. Firefighters built the entire office and oft area of the station.

The two agencies were housed in separate facilities before this building was built, even though a lot of gear and equipment was shared by the mostly "same" firefighters. The geographic center location of the City of St. John made it the logical position for the county to house specialized equipment/trucks. This was not possible with the two small truck bays that were available before.

The total cost of this project was just over $121,000. Salvaged items from the annex building helped defray the cost of the new building.

NEW RESCUE TOOLS

Until recently Stafford County's rescue tools came to you via an old ambulance, a utility truck, a pumper, and a trailer. That all changed when a custom rescue truck was purchased. The new rescue truck replaced the utility truck.

The plan is to purchase specialized rescue tools for the new rescue truck – ones we couldn't possibly afford to outfit on all four rescue units. This plan took an unexpected catapult forward through the generosity of local Stafford County resident Carl Dudrey.

What happened was Dudrey became aware of a new line of rescue tools – tools that have some unique features. First, the tools were said to have the strongest cutting power of any rescue tool on the market. Second, the tools have the capability of quickly changing the tips. Dudrey was sold and offered to purchase the tools if Stafford County firefighters wanted them.

The reason added strength is important with rescue tools is because new vehicles are being built with metals that are far stronger than

they've ever been. To prove or disprove that point, Stafford firefighters put the new tools – Champion Tools – to the test, using them side-by-side with existing tools.

Station Chief Jerry Sanders said, "The Champion tool was far superior. When the existing tool stalled in its track, the Champion tool never hesitated a bit."

Interchangeability isn't necessarily a feature that all firefighters believe in when it comes to rescue tools. With time being so critical, firefighters worry that changing the tips on rescue tools will steal away valuable time. So, Stafford firefighters also put this feature to the test.

Assistant Chief Shon Meschberger provided the feedback. Shon said, "Changing the tips took a maximum of eight seconds." He also believes that a little bit of lubrication could even make the process faster. Furthermore, Shon stressed the importance of making all the cuts you anticipate with one tool tip before switching to another.

The Stafford County Fire Department sincerely appreciates Carl Dudrey's generosity, and they are excited about having the new equipment. While nobody hopes to use rescue tools, it's comforting to know they are there if the need should arise.

A LOLLIPOP MOMENT

I don't know the number of long distant ambulance transfers I have taken in my life – let's just say the number is high. I've learned a lot about life during these trips. A recent one was from Stafford Hospital to Great Bend Regional.

The patient was a retired firefighter named – Joe Reboul. During the trip, Joe and I talked about his life experience – mostly about his career.

Joe was in the Navy and served during the Korean War. I asked him if he liked that time and his comment was, "Oh Yea!"

The next stop in Joe's career was the fire service. I asked Joe what advice he would give a young person wanting a career in the fire service. His reply – "Don't do it!" But he was just kidding.

Joe said, "It takes a pretty special person to be a firefighter – and it aint' for everybody." Joe said that he would do it all again if given the chance.

The first fire truck Joe rode in was an Old Red Seagraves – an open cab model. As a matter of fact, when Joe came to the fire department, all the fire trucks were open cab style.

The most memorable incident Joe could recall was a house fire in Arlington back in the 60's. Two children perished in the basement of that house.

Then there were the two babies he helped deliver. The first was delivered in the front yard. Unfortunately, this was a house fire and the mother had been rescued but succumbed to the fire. Luckily, the baby survived.

The second baby was born in the back seat of a car. Both mother and baby made it through that "outside the hospital childbirth experience" in flying colors.

During that trip to Great Bend, Joe gave me a "Lollipop Moment." Let me explain.

I watched a short presentation the other day by a man named Drew Dudley. Drew's message was that – "Every day, unbeknownst to us, we impact somebody in a wonderful way." He called it "everyday leadership" and he gave the moment that this happens a name – "A Lollipop Moment."

Joe passed away several days ago. Before he left, he gave many of us a "lollipop moment" – many more than he would ever know. I was the recipient of one.

"Thanks' for the lollipop Joe – we'll miss you."

A NEW STAFFORD VOICE

Davin Graves has posted his very first story on the "new" Stafford County Emergency Service site. I am honored by that story being about me.

Please visit it and set up a link.

Davin is much too humble about his writing ability. Big words really aren't all that important. What is most important is the heart. This young man has one of the biggest.

And it shows in his words.

Enjoy!

MAKING LEMONADE

Last fall the Stafford County Fire Department lost a mini-brush truck in a fire that burned 700 acres before it was contained. If you run a business, you're going to have occasional losses. Emergency service is no different. When you have a loss, you try to learn something from it, and you move on. That's what we did.

In moving on we discovered that we could take the lemon – the burned truck – and turn it into lemonade.

The insurance settlement for the burned truck was $43,000. Before they settled with us, they offered to sell the entire burned truck for $3,500. We quickly accepted the offer since there was little damage to the rear portion of the truck.

We then looked at the Fire Department's primary needs. A rescue truck was the top need identified.

Currently, rescue operations for the county come from Macksville, St. John, Stafford, and Seward. The tools are carried on: an old orange ambulance in Macksville, a Class "A" pumper in St. John, an old model truck with a rusty utility bed in Stafford (see side picture), and a pull behind trailer in Seward.

None of the current rescue units are large enough to carry all the specialized equipment that might be needed for a rescue. Moreover, it doesn't make fiscal sense to buy four large trucks and all the specialized equipment (even if we had funds to do so). But it does make sense to buy one. And that's exactly what we did.

We found a rescue truck that fit our needs perfectly. With insurance monies available we made the $19,000 purchase. Since the Stafford station has the strongest 24/7 staffing of available fire personnel, the decision was made to house the truck there. We will purchase additional specialized equipment as the budget allows.

Another decision we had to make was whether we would replace the burned rescue truck. We had the slightly burned truck bed and we also had a low mileage truck that was being used as a water transfer unit. So, the decision was made to repair the burned truck's bed and place it on the water transfer truck. The water transfer trucks' bed will be moved to the old Stafford rescue truck, keeping that truck in service.

The cost of putting the brush truck back together was made less expensive through the generosity of firefighters. Shon Meschberger, Shane Meschberger, Jerry Sanders, Larry Sanders, and others from the Stafford Station fixed the damage to the brush truck at no cost to the County. The only expenses were $300 for parts.

We will have the lime truck painted red to match the bed. This will be done by an auto body shop at a cost of $1,000.

Total cost for replacing the brush truck: $3,500 + $1,000 + $300 = $4,800. This expense added to the expense of the rescue truck brought our grand total to $23,000.

Next on our needs' list was the need to refurbish a Water Tanker/Tender at the Hudson Station. This truck has a sound chassis, but the

tank is leaking. Additionally, the truck isn't designed with all the features that a tanker/tender should have. Bids were secured for this work, as well as a $5,000 state grant. Minus the grant the total cost of the refurbishment was $11,676.

Adding in the refurbishment cost brings the total monies spent to $33,676 – still well under the $43,000 insurance monies received.

Sometimes, it's possible to turn a bad thing into a good thing – especially when you incorporate the generosity of donated labor. The Stafford County Fire Department is appreciative of the support "YOU the CITIZENS" give us. We pledge to do our best to keep our operation fiscally and operationally responsible.

NEW AMBULANCE

Stafford County received a new ambulance. The ambulance manufacturer was American Response Vehicles out of Columbia, Missouri. The cost was $121,000 with the trade-in. This unit will replace an ambulance that had over 130,000 miles and had recently been taken out of service because of mechanical problems.

The ambulance will initially be placed in the City of St. John but will be available for all long-distance transfers. Once we're sure that we don't have warranty issues, the ambulance will take a back line position. This will ensure that we maximize the usage of our fleet.

The ambulance will be brought to each of the upcoming EMS crew meetings but stop by the station and. look at it if you get a chance.

NEW GENERATOR

Stafford County took possession of a new portable 40 KW generator.

Counties throughout Kansas acquired the generators through a state grant. The generator's price tag was over $23,000.

The purpose of the generators is to provide emergency power to critical infrastructures during emergencies.

Each county is required to make the generator available to other Kansas counties, if there should be a need; and they don't need the generator for emergency purposes in their county.

ANNIE, ARE YOU OKAY?

There she is lying motionless on the carpeted floor. The young lady appears to be around twenty years old. Her skin is a pale color. She is a thin lady with straight blond hair that's rather course. She must be an athlete, because she's wearing a blue polyester athletic suit – both jacket and pants.

A man nearby tells you the lady's name is Annie. As you kneel beside her, you gently shake her and ask her – *"Annie Are You OK? So, Annie Are You OK? Are You OK, Annie? Annie Are You OK?"* And, there's no reply.

You lean over with your head turning as you do, so your ear is close by to her nose and mouth. As you listen for her breathing you look for any chest rise. There is none. You encircle her mouth with yours and you blow several times.

Then you place the tips of one of your hands' fingers upon Annie's throat and then slide them slightly down her neck. You feel for any faint pulsation. There is none.

You grab the zipper of her jacket and pull it down to discover she's wearing nothing underneath. You place one of your hands over your other and interlock your fingers. Then your palm is placed on Annie's chest. With arms straight you push down – repeatedly.

How long you have worked in emergency medical service determines if your first CPR was done on Annie. Your first might have been one with another name, but Annie was the first. And that might have been why Michael Jackson chose her when he wrote the lyrics for his song *"Smooth Criminal."*

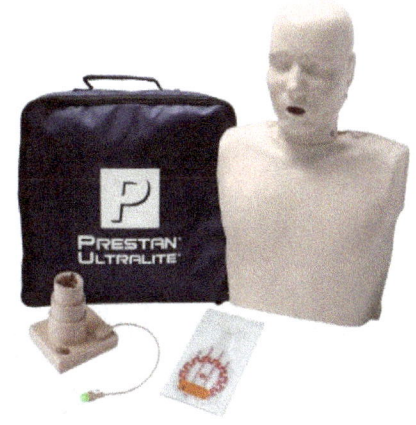

As I watched the documentary about Michael Jackson this

evening it amazed me the greatness of this man. He studied the greats in every single category that his work touched. And he brought the best of them together to make his magic.

I never knew the key words of *"Smooth Criminal"* were derived from a training manikin phrase, nor did I know the story of how his music and videos were produced.

Those of us in emergency service should play this song whenever we train. It could remind us to seek the same greatness in what we do, as did the great Michael Jackson.

Aaow!!!

NEW STATION CHIEF

Tom Fischer was chosen as the new Stafford County Station Chief for the Hudson Station Tom was instrumental in getting County State Firemen's Relief Association back on track. This means thousands of dollars more received for the County's firefighters. He also had a financial planner visit one-on-one with each of the firefighters.

Tom is also a Deputy with the Sheriff's office.

He will take over duties immediately.

EMERGENCY OPERATIONS CENTER

The time is getting closer. After the construction of the new fire station (and moving the fire trucks from the EMS/Fire station) the two bays in the old station are being remodeled into an Emergency Operations Center.

Blocks were laid in the bay door openings. Interior walls were built by emergency crews. Insulation will also be installed by emergency per-

sonnel. Professionals will be hired to complete the electrical, heating, and air conditioning.

Many components of the construction project were salvaged from the annex project. This list includes the ceiling tile

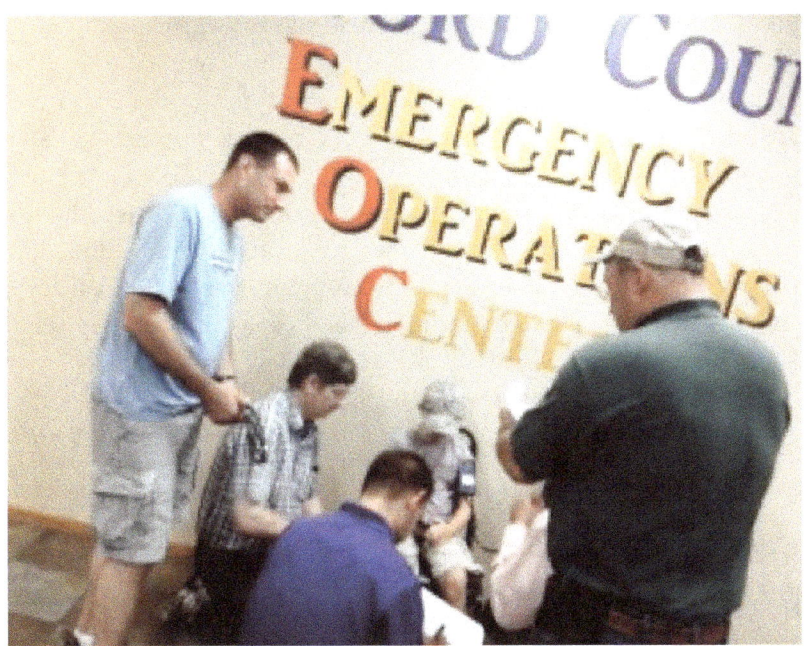

system, doors, sheet rock, ceiling fans, lights, cabinets, and trim. The entire cost of the project is being paid for with memorial funds that were donated to the department.

It was a sparse crowd that showed up for the Emergency Operation Center "Open House" yesterday. That was somewhat expected.

First, emergency responders usually focus on what they see that directly impacts them. Items such as trucks and equipment are visible, easy to identify resources. You can't extinguish a fire without a fire truck and fire hose. And you can't take care of a sick person without a cot and an ambulance.

Next is the public. The public probably scratch their heads and wonder, "What the heck is an Emergency Operation Center." And honestly a room with radios and multi-media equipment doesn't excite one's curiosity.

This apparent lack of interest might explain why Stafford County has never had an Emergency Operation Center. It also might explain why our dispatchers have such meager quarters. But it's a mistaken lack of focus.

If you watched the television documentary on the World Trade Center terrorist attacks last night you saw that one of the problems – which seems to be a problem with any large-scale incident – is communications. The deficiency resulted in the loss of life – many.

The EOC will provide Stafford County with a key

improvement in communications. I pointed out (to the group that attended the open house) that Stafford County is fortunate to have some very thoughtful residents.

Long time Stafford County resident Ina Maye Toland left the fire department monies (in her will) that paid for the entire EOC. Just recently there was another Stafford County resident who paid for a complete complement of rescue tools. Things like this rarely happen in larger communities.

If you didn't make it to the Open House, it's not too late. It's located at 636 E. 4th St. in St. John. We won't have any cake left, but we'll brew you a cup of coffee.

HUDSON – RESCUED BY MISTY

It was a head-on collision that should've killed both drivers and both dogs on board. But miraculously neither the two men, nor the two dogs were killed. Unfortunately, one of the dogs – we will call her Hudson, suffered a broken leg.

A quick call to the veterinarian in Great Bend estimated the cost to treat the dog would be around $600. The owner gave orders to euthanatize the young pup. In steps Paramedic Misty who would take the dog,

Meanwhile, I called my son, Matthew, who is a media computer expert, for help. Matthew posted the story on the Internet along with a request for donations to cover Hudson's medical care.

Before Misty could pay the medical bill, Matthew had donations to cover the entire cost.

Several months later, Deputy/Volunteer Fire Chief Tom Fischer adopted Hudson. All kinds of great people step forward to save a seriously injured puppy.

NEW ST. JOHN CITY FIRE CHIEF

St. John City Fire Chief Leonard Getty announced his retirement Tuesday evening at the City Council meeting.

Assistant Fire Chief Mike Sanders was appointed to replace Chief Getty.

Congratulations to both!

DON'T SHOOT YOUR EYE OUT

I'm sure my sons loathed having a firefighter as a father when Independence Day rolled around each year. Yes, I'm a self- professed, proverbial "stick in the mud" when it comes to shooting fireworks. I also understand I could be a bit biased on the matter. And, for that reason I don't expect everyone – or many at all – to agree with me on this matter.

But I wouldn't be properly fulfilling my role as a Fire Chief if I didn't say a few words about fireworks safety – beginning with a story.

This story took place on a beautiful sunny day about 22 years ago today.

A group of young teens were at Milford State Lake getting geared up for a fun holiday weekend. Adding to the fun, one of the boys had brought his parent's rag top Jeep.

Like most young people – and some older folks too – the boys hadn't done much preplanning. They had forgotten to stock up on food and drinks. So, they decided to make a run to the convenience store. On that trip they drove by a firework stand.

Plenty of beverages and munchies were bought and placed into the Jeep (the top was up). On their way back to the campsite they decided to check out the prices at the firework stand. The prices were incred-

ible. They were able to purchase enough pyrotechnics to put on a small-town public display.

The Jeep was carefully packed – boys, beverages, munchies, and fireworks.

One of the boys – in the front passenger's seat – was smoking a cigarette as they made their way back to the campsite. The boys talked and laughed as the cigarette burned towards the butt. Then, the smoker flicked the butt – towards the open window. Only, the butt hit the wind and made a quick U-turn – right into the back seat area – unbeknownst to anyone.

The popping of a large flat of Black Cats was official notice that the friends had a problem. For a moment the driver thought it was just a prank and kept driving. But the first flat of fireworks progressed to another, and another, and another. Before the Jeep could be stopped the entire arsenal was exploding. And the Jeep was on fire.

All the boys were taken to a local hospital by ambulance. Two were transferred on to the St. Francis burn unit in Wichita. All the boys survived. But, celebrating July 4th – for them – was forever changed.

So, there's the story. I could tell others – all true accounts of tragedy tied to fireworks. But I don't want to belabor my message. Furthermore, I'm not an advocate of sheltering ourselves – or our loved ones – from every risk in life. To do so would make for a very bland, boring, life. What I do advocate is to take prudent precautions when one is living life on the edge.

You've all read the bullet point lists of firework dos and don'ts, so I won't regurgitate them. My message is simple. "Use common sense."

Have a fun, safe Independence Day – and God Bless America!

FATALITY AUTO ACCIDENT

Stafford County Firefighters work a fatality accident on Highway 281 & K-19.

This was the second fatality to occur at this location in less than 2 months.

Firefighters used their full complement of rescue tools that a Stafford County businessman paid for completely.

PAWS FOR PREVENTION

Howdy Partners! (Hola Companeros – for you Spanish children.) Dalmatians might be the American fire mascot, but they're big like adults. I'm not black and white. And, I don't have any spots. What I am is a little fellow just like you kids. And being little I can see things from your viewpoint.

My name is Felipe Carlito Rodriguez – FCR for short. Stafford County Emergency Service Director Steve Moody's son Weston Moody brought me to the United States from my hometown of Guadalajara, Mexico.

Steve Moody – nice guy that he is – offered me a monthly spot on his blog to talk to you about prevention. So, here goes my first message – "Monkey See Monkey Do".

I believe your parents taught you well and you have a pretty good idea of what's right and what's wrong – what's safe and what's unsafe. The problem happens when you get together with one of your friends – it might even be your brother or sister – and you ignore your brain telling you what your parents taught you.

The big people have a fancy name for it called "Peer Pressure."

If you have even a little bit of doubt whether doing something is safe or not, then it's NOT. No matter how much I teach you about prevention – staying safe – those lessons can easily be forgotten when you get together with your friends. It might even be YOU that suggests doing something you know is wrong.

The reason they call it Monkey See Monkey Do is because monkeys tend to get into all kinds of mischief.

So, if you are ever with a friend and he or she suggests doing something that seems remotely unsafe – picture the MONKEY and say to yourself – "I'm no Monkey!"

This is FCR signing off.

Remember – "Ten Cuidado – STAY SAFE!"

PUMP 3

The young man drives up to "Short Stop Fuel" and parks his beat up 4-door late- model Chevy next to the fuel pump – just as he ran out of gas. The forlorn subject steps out of his car, walks across to the store, and up to the check-out counter. He hands the clerk a debit card and says, "$5.00 on Pump 3."

The clerk swipes the card, and the machine flashes the message "Rejected." By now there's a young lady and two men in line behind him. The clerk again swipes the card. And again, it comes back "Rejected." Embarrassed, he takes the card and returns to his gas empty car.

The young lady – who didn't know the gas-needy man – steps forward to the counter. She lays her items for purchase on the counter. As the clerk is ringing up the charge she says, "I also want you to put $20.00 on Pump 3."

Acts such as these are a regular event in small towns in America. Just weeks ago, a late-night storm dropped tornadoes onto farms in rural Stafford County. At least six of those farms were totally devastated.

Before the sun had crept above the horizon they arrived. They brought their trucks. They brought their trailers. They brought their food. And they brought their hearts.

It's just one of the special things about rural America. The good deeds might go unnoticed by many, but they didn't go unnoticed by the

THE STORY OF MY LIFE

storm ravaged victims, nor the young man on "Pump 3."

REFLECTING ON 34 YEARS
A look back in Time. Available online @ Amazon.com chiefmoody55.

It all started 66 years ago. Kansas was going through a sweltering heat wave with prolonged temperatures well into the triple digits. I was told that it was so hot many Kansans were talking about climate change, but I don't know that for sure. It was my first day on earth.

Sixty-six years is a long, long, long time – and much has happened. Historic events, natural disasters, classic movies, music to dance to, invenJons, wars, many have leg us, and many have been born. Can a sixty-six-year-old reJred fire chief with thirty-seven years' experience share some reflections worth reading? I'll give it a shot.

Never lose your zest and happiness for life. One of my personal favorite career pictures was this one. My administraJve assistant in Leavenworth,

Cary Collins, a wonderful person, took the picture during a fire prevenJon visit. The children's faces say it all. When I occasionally let a bit of negativity enter my mind, I pull out this picture. It's all it takes to get back on track. Find your reminder.

NEVER STOP LEARNING
You can learn from people – all people. You can learn from watching a movie. You can learn from listening to a speaker, or a musician. You can learn by reading. You can learn by playing a game. Learn with your total body – your mind, your heart, and your soul. When you stop learning you are done. A picture of my emergency responders is my reminder of what's at stake. Find your reminder.

TREAT EVERYONE WITH RESPECT
Everyone must make some tough choices in life. You don't have to love everyone you meet, but you can respect them. CriJcize ideas not people. I personally knew I had it figured out one day when I terminated

an employee for just cause – but did it respec`ully – and he apologized to me aJerwards.

SomeJmes employing the "never stop learning" makes you a bit too smart for your britches. A short passage from an old movie named "Harvey" is my reminder. *"My grandmother always told me, "In this world Stevie – she always called me Stevie – in this world Stevie, you must be oh so smart or oh so pleasant. For years I was smart, I recommend pleasant. You may quote me."* Find your reminder.

GIVE THANKS TO OTHERS

Nobody is self-made – nobody. Help comes in different servings from different people. Have you thanked your boss or your workers? Have you thanked your spouse, your parents, your children, your friends, your customers. A picture of my wife helps remind me. Find your reminder.

THE LUCKIEST MAN

Many people don't know about my love for the *"Game of Baseball"*. I liken it to my love for the *"Game of Emergency Service"*.

In baseball my favorite player was a man named Lou Gehrig. This player was dealt what he called "a bad blow" (a fatal disease) that forced him from his career and took his life shortly thereafter.

Gehrig gave an epic speech at Yankee Stadium to tell everyone about his situation. I'm not trying to compare myself to Gehrig, but

I modified his speech to tie it into the ending chapter of my time in Stafford County.

Folks, for the past several weeks you have been reading about the bad break I got. Yet today I consider myself the **"Luckiest Man on the Face of the Earth."** Let me explain.

I have worked in Fire & EMS for the past 35 years. I have received more than my fair share of kindness and encouragement from my fellow workers and customers during those years.

Just look at the grand men and women I have worked with over the years and now lately. Which of you wouldn't consider it the highlight of his or her career just to associate with them for even one day? Sure, I'm lucky.

On the fire side who wouldn't consider it an honor to have worked with Jerry Sanders and Marshal Sanders along with the Stafford and St. John firefighters? How about those up north – Tom Fisher and Mark Clasen along with their firefighters? And then on the west side is Rob Murrow with his Macksville firefighters.

On the EMS side you have Jorja Coleman leading the Stafford EMTs, Misty Blakeslee leading St. John, and Gregg Maseberg with the lead for Macksville. Then there's St. John Police Chief Adam Sayler, Macksville Police Chief Troy Wright, and Stafford Police Chief Doug Brown who performs every emergency role ever invented.

And let us not forget the three administrative officers who must put up with me more than any of the others. These three – Misty Blakeslee, Nick Lauffer and Davin Graves – they accomplish so much behind the scenes.

And one of my favorites that does a bit of everything – the little energizer bunny named Brenda.

And this doesn't even include the greats during my career in Salina and Leavenworth, nor our incredible partners at the hospital and the dispatch room – it's a list that could go on and on. Surely, I'm lucky.

When you have parents who work so that you can eat, stay warm, and get an education – it's a blessing. When you have a wife who has been a tower of strength and shown more courage than you dreamed existed – that's the finest I know,

A NEW STAFFORD VOICE

Davin Graves has posted his very first story on the "new" Stafford County Emergency Service site. I am honored by that story being about me.

Please visit it and set up a link.

Davin is much too humble about his wriJng ability. Big words really aren't all that important. What is most important is the heart. This young man has one of the biggest.

And it shows in his words. Enjoy!

A WAY WITH WORDS

Story by Davin Graves

In the last two weeks of Director Moody's presence at Stafford County, there were multiple conversations that ensued. One of those conversations consisted of discussing the need to keep you, the public, informed in the ongoings of Emergency Services.

Which brings us to the point of this blog. Steve discussed with me the possibility of continuing the blog that he was so well-known for. This was a large task to take on since I was very aware, and you will be too, that I was nowhere close to as good of a writer as he was.

However, Steve was a man of little doubt and assured me the more I wrote the more it would enhance my writing abilities. Though I did not want to simply take over the blog that he had built up, due to a

majority wanting to continue to follow his stories, we did elect to develop a similar blog.

Out of all the blogs that I read and the stories that we listened to from Steve, it did not take long to learn that the man had a way with words. At times during a story the need was there to interrupt him simply to clarify what a word meant. There is a very simple explanation as to why he was so fluent with words.

Many years ago, Steve encountered an individual that liked to use large words. He found this very frustrating and so he developed a plan to solve the problem. As time went on, every time that he was reading a book or conversing and a word that he was unfamiliar with came up, he wrote it down. He would then later make an index card for the word and whenever he had time, he would study the "stacks of cards." From that point on whenever that individual used a large word, Steve would reply right back with his own large word — problem solved.

An attempt will be made at keeping you informed about what is going on in Emergency Services. Just please bear with me as my stack of index cards is still very small.

HAIL TO THE CHIEF

Commissioners officially made Misty Blakeslee Interim EMS Director.

If a Director/Chief does his/her job right, then he will prepare his next-in-line to take over the lead position when he leaves.

It's an honor to me that I played a role in the development of Misty to take over the Director position.

So, we will *"Hail to the Interim."*

Get the Interim word out soon.

THE STAFFORD ENDING

In many ways a person's life is somewhat like a story book. You have the introduction, followed by the body, followed by the closing.

The chapters within the sections will likely be different. And that word different is an understatement for describing the past few weeks in my book.

At one point it looked as though I was going to be unemployed for the first time in my life. Then it looked as though things would be worked out. Then maybe they wouldn't. Then it was back to hopeful again.

The hope only happened because a group of people cared enough to support me. That support was something few people get to experience in their lifetime.

Just as it seemed like things were settling back to normal, I got a call last week from a representative from the City of Eldorado. They wanted to interview me for their fire chief opening.

As you might recall, I submitted my resignation at two Commissioner's meetings, despite the incredible support, because my head told me it was the best thing to do. When given the chance – twice – to stay, my heart convinced my head to rescind my resignation.

The thought of being unemployed might have also helped the heart override the head. And you can probably guess where this is going.

I was offered and accepted the position of Eldorado Fire Chief. My last day as Stafford County Emergency Service Director will be October 11th.

I have offered to assist Stafford County not just up to this date – I have offered to assist Stafford County "long distance", in whatever way I can, for the rest of my life.

The Stafford County chapters in my life book will be some of my "Most Treasured." Thank you for giving me the opportunity to be a part of your book.

God Speed, I love you all.

Stafford County – Simply the Best!

CHAPTER 5
MY CAREER IN ELDORADO

THE BEGINNING
Like most fire departments the El Dorado fire department was a proud group of men and women. But sometimes it takes a view from an outside fire chief to see things that could use some improvement. The culture of the El Dorado fire department was something we addressed. Next was a review along with some updates to SOGs.

Partnerships were something else that needed to be improved – Butler Community College, a professional photographer named Chad Wittenberg, Holly Frontier Refinery.

Evaluated the department's reporting system. Methods of recognizing firefighters needed addressed. Equipment needed to be evaluated with an aerial truck at the top of the needs list. Top level outside training was another thing to be encouraged.

So, here we go with showcasing some of the things we accomplished in my 3 ½ years with the department.

GETTING TO KNOW YOUR FIREFIGHTERS
"I started the practice of profiling my firefighters" when I was in Salina and have carried it on to Leavenworth, Stafford County, and in El Dorado. It's a wonderful way to get to know your firefighters.

I began working with the El Dorado Fire Department in October of 2013. I began my adventure in the fire service as a firefighter with the Salina Fire Department in 1978. I worked up through the ranks and served as Deputy Chief from 1996 until my departure in 2006.

I then went on to be the Fire Chief for the Leavenworth Fire Department from 2006 until 2009. In 2009 I moved west to become Emergency Service Director in Stafford County until 2013.

I was born and raised in Salina, Kansas. After graduating from Salina High School, I attended Hutchinson Community College completing an Associates of Applied Science Degree in Emergency Medical Services, where I obtained my Paramedic certification. I continued my education attending K- State completing a bachelor's degree in technology management in 2001. I'm also a Certified Public Manager, Certified Emergency Manager, and have completed the National Fire Academy's Executive Fire Officer Program

I married my high school sweetheart, Rosie. We have two sons Matthew and Weston. Our oldest, Matthew is married to his wife Erin, and they have three children - Macoy, Vienna, and Lenon. Weston, the youngest, is married to his wife Kiley and they have two children as well, Amaia and Grayson.

I would say one of my greatest career accomplishments as El Dorado Fire Chief was: overseeing the three groups: the paid firefighters, the volunteers\reserves, and the students.

VOLUNTEER FF OF THE YEAR

His name is Rodney Reed. This man was recognized this past Saturday as the *"Eldorado Volunteer Firefighter of the Year."* And to make things even more special – if that's possible – this wasn't the first time he'd received the award. Rodney also received the award in 2011.

Continuing the special things is how long Rodney has served as a volunteer firefighter. This coming February it will be 20 years. When asked what attracted him to becoming a firefighter Rodney said, *"I followed in my dad and uncle's footsteps."* His dad served 20 years and was also a recipient of the same award. And his uncle was a 25-year firefighter.

The award is based upon three criteria. The first benchmark is *"Number of Calls."* Rodney responded to 38 structure fire calls for the year. Next on the list is *"Time Put in at the Fire Station."* Last, is *"Attendance at Training."* Rodney made every single training meeting.

When asked about the most memorable fire in his career Rodney quickly named the Old Town Pizza fire in the 100 Block of South Main.

Rodney was the first volunteer on scene and was part of the first entry team. His partners were Captain (later to become Chief) Nakaten, and Driver Jack Zimmerman. They made entry and tried to get a knockdown, but the fire was more advanced than they realized. After hearing ventilation units start dropping to the floor in the next room over, they knew it was time to vacate the building. The building ended up being a total loss as was the building next door.

Rodney's wife Gaylene was present to hear Volunteer Liaison Lieutenant Coby Spear make the winning announcement. Rodney said of Spear, *"He's one of the best Liaison Officers we have had – a Great Trainer!"*

There's another pretty great person and that's FF Rodney Reed. Congratulations Rodney and *"Thank You"* for your dedicated service!

130 YEARS OF PRIDE IN SERVICE -

Story by Captain Jellison

On July 31st of 2015, FDNY celebrated 150 years as an organized fire department. They had multiple volunteer departments prior to that date, but July 31st was when a New York State Act created a paid, unified fire department for the City of New York.

This is significant today because El Dorado celebrated a similar anniversary. The City of El Dorado was incorporated on September 12, 1871. Then on April 2nd, 1885, a fire department was organized to protect the citizens who called El Dorado home. So, the El Dorado Fire Department celebrated 130 years of Pride in service!

It is impressive to think that the oil field boom town that became El Dorado had organized a fire department only 20 years after the organization of FDNY! We really were a progressive community in those times!

LEGENDARY EFD FIRE CHIEF RALPH GREEN

Long term EFD Fire Chief Ralph Green retiree died from an accidental death. Our thoughts go out to Chief Green's wife and family.

On-duty crews, as well as off-duty firefighters, attended the service. Several other County departments covered the city during the Services.

And it's a good thing they did because midway through the services crews were paged to respond to an emergency.

1ST FEMALE FIRE SCIENCE LIVE-IN

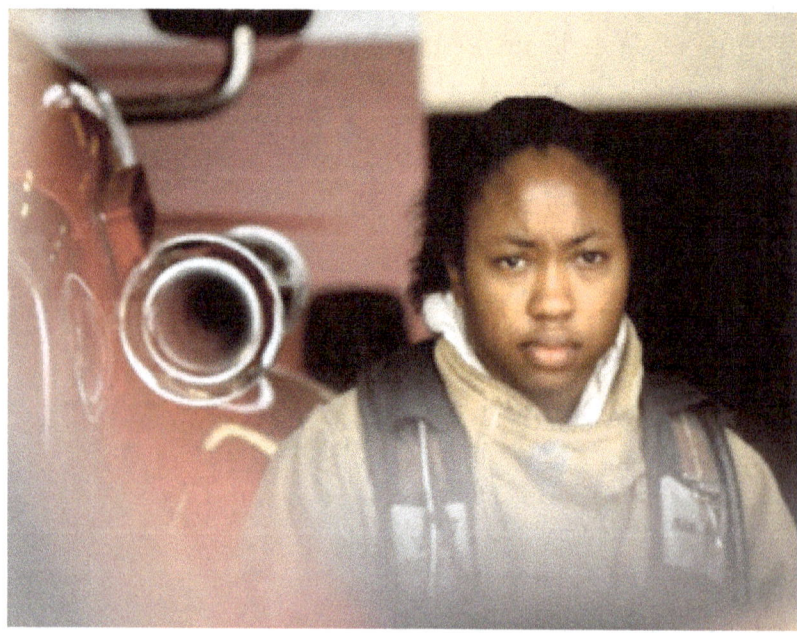

I proudly welcomed the department's first female live-in from Butler Community College.

Welcome aboard!

SOGS & ANNUAL BOOKS - BLOG

Chief Joe Haag is a brilliant man, with many skills. I started the blog and the writing of the annual book when I arrived in El Dorado. Joe took over both jobs and did so better than what I did.

We both had the assistance from Photographer Chad Wittenberg's pictures.

The annual report – called "The Year in Review" was a method of communicating with the three department groups – paid, volunteers, and fire science students.

In addition, the Blog served to communicate with the public.

EL DORADO FIREFIGHTERS MDA DRIVE

It was the final day of the Muscular Dystrophy fund drive. The El Dorado Fire Department has participated in this event as far back as one can remember. Children afflicted by this disease are helped by funds collected.

Hopefully, one day there will be a cure, but just to know that kids live better and live longer because of the funds collected – well, that made it all worthwhile. American's dig deep into their pockets when asked to support a worthy cause, but few equal the citizens of El Dorado. The three-day total was $4,850.

Thank you, citizens of El Dorado. You are the best!

SEVERAL GREAT OFFICERS

There are many "Great Men" on the El Dorado fire department, but I'll just identify two officers.

The first is Troy Jellison. Troy was a shift commander overseeing operations for both station's firefighters, volunteers, and the fire science students.

Troy has taken numerous fire courses, but the pinnacle of his leadership programs under his belt is the Executive Fire Officer program through the National Fire Academy in Emmittsburg, Maryland. The course consists of four two-week campus courses with a research paper as a follow-up to each class. The paper is required to be master's degree level that hits all the research guidelines.

A professor grades each research paper, and it is sent back for revision if it doesn't meet all the requirements.

Only a small number of candidates are selected from the number of applicants. I had to write a recommendation letter that explained how the job of company officer in El Dorado reflects the title of Battalion Chief.

There are only a small number of EFO graduates in the nation.

The second person is Fire Chief Joe Haag. Upon my departure Joe took over the chief's position of the El Dorado Fire Chief.

It makes me proud that the City Manager chose an internal candidate to fill the position. Joe is highly qualified to fill the role.

Joe has taken a multitude of fire related classes. But the pinnacle of his education was a master's degree that he completed while I was serving as chief.

Joe was an incredible Assistant Chief. He wrote SOGs that were professionally published. Also, he was the major writer of the annual reports.

He also took over for me the writing of a "Year in Review" books for the annual dinner get together. Joe is one of the "Great Men."

PARTNERSHIPS

First on the list of partnerships in need of improvement was Holly Frontier Refinery. I started a monthly lunch meeting with their chief fire department representative Dave Zorn.

The refinery is contiguous with the City of El Dorado, and they have their own fire department on their grounds. Their gear, equipment, and trucks are top notch. We started having training sessions with their men on the refinery grounds.

I was able to get the refinery to cover the expense of sending six different teams of two to Texas for state-of-the art refinery fire training.

A SUPER PHOTOGRAPHER

Next on the list of partnerships was a photographer. At each of the departments I worked in, we established a close friendship with the local photographer, I found the one for El Dorado simply by happenstance.

His name is Chad Wittenberg and we met one day on a house fire. He was a professional photographer and was just taking pictures of our house fire freelance.

I asked Chad if he would like to serve as the El Dorado fire department photographer. We would outfit him with a safety vest, an official ID, and a radio. He would be a part of the team. The only thing was we didn't have budgeted funds to pay him.

He would have to post his pictures on his website to sale them. He said, "yes." What we got was one of the most incredible pictures one could imagine. Chad's pictures were used by the State Fire marshal's office and several fire service magazines.

THANKSGIVING AND THE ISLAND OF MISFIT TOYS

The other day my wife and I were sitting on the front porch enjoying what I called the "Perfect Day." Just then my wife noticed the tiniest cloud drifting across the completely blue sky. I turned to my wife and said, "Almost Perfect."

It was a joke.

Imperfections are really what makes life so special. And that is what I'm thankful for on this upcoming day of Thanksgiving. Let me explain.

One of my favorite holiday movies is the low-budget film "Rudolph the Red-nosed Reindeer and the Island of Misfit Toys."

I suppose a reason for my connection is my own imperfections. One happened when I was a child. I contracted polio and was severely affected on the right side of my body. Most noticeable is my right leg that's one and one-half inches shorter.

Anyhow, the movie begins by drawing attention to the shameful treatment doled out to those who are different from the rest of the crowd.

Rudolph meets up with an elf named Hermey. Both Rudolph and Hermey are misfits. The two run away from home and end up on the Island of Unwanted Toys.

The beauty of the show is when it concludes by showing how being different is not necessarily a bad thing, in fact it can be a wonderful thing.

We strive to be the best we can be and that's not bad. But, sometimes in our effort to reach perfection, we lose sight of how an imperfection can also be special.

I hope Americans take the time to watch this short movie. And, afterwards, ask yourself if you need to do a little bit better at seeing the good in those who are a bit different.

It might even make you happier – and thankful.

"AFTER THE FIRE"

EL DORADO Fire Department Photographer Chad Wittenberg photo. Pictured is an early 2.00 a.m. fire that burned three houses.

Chad arrived on scene right alongside firefighters

One can almost smell, feel, and see the "Aftermath of Fire.

Thanks Chad.

ELDORADO TOWER RIBBING CUTTING

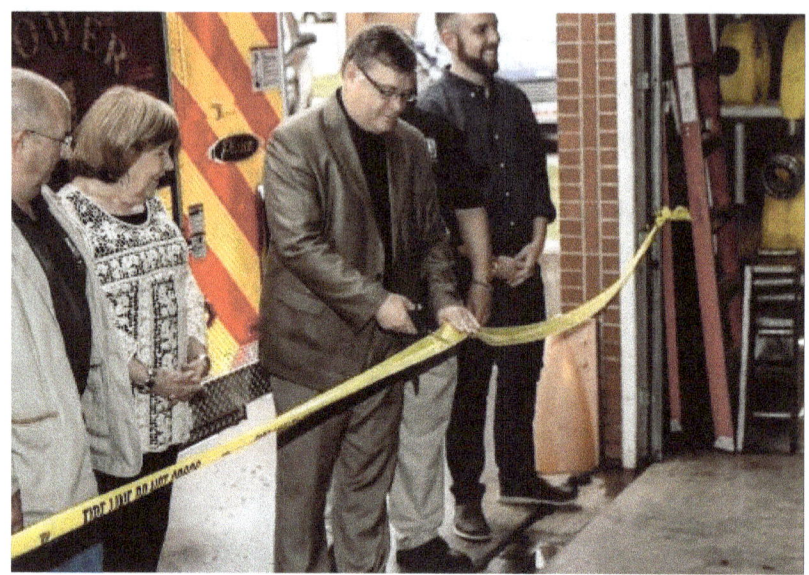

Here stands the Mayor, accompanied by the rest of the El Dorado City Commissioners.

They stand reeady to "Cut the Ribbon" as a standing tradition for "newly acquired fire trucks.

Tower 1 is a beautiful addition to El Dorado's fleet of fire apparatus.

The Tower came in at a cost of a smooth million dollars.

PICTURE PORTRAIT PRISONER SHOW CASES

Changing out employee pictures when firefighters leave and when they arrive can be a real pain in the backside. It's also difficult to keep pictures the same size. So, we assigned Firefighter Roger Newell to come up with a design and hire a company to make the dream come true.

What Roger came up with was a beautiful 5' by 8' oak showcase. Along the inside of the frame was a ¼" groove. The groove was used to slide a full glass front, in and out, to update the pitchers.

Three rubber, round suction cups,

with handles, were used to lift into and out of placement. The backside of the case was embroidered "Salina Fire Department." Firefighters and Public loved the case.

I think it's important to display the firefighters currently with the department. Retirees also had a spot in the show case.

Well, I told myself that if I became Fire Chief at another fire department that I would do my best to make a portrait case like Salinas. First stop was Leavenworth. The only problem I ran into right away was the cost. The cost was around $1,400. That was going to be a problem because our budget didn't allow it.

I've never been one who gives up easily when faced with a problem. When I met with all the key personnel in Leavenworth upon my arrival, I found out the State Prison has a fully equipped woodworking shop.

I asked the Warden if they could build us a portrait show case that matched Salinas. And not only did they build one, but the only cost to my fire department was the cost of materials.

Six years later the Warden did it again. He had prisoners build another show case for me in El Dorado. I wish I could have put another picture of the prisoners on the wall. Prison rules prohibited it though.

So, we did the next best thing. A picture of the prisoner's hands aside an American flag. Men make mistakes in life and sometimes the mistakes mean jail time. But it doesn't mean these men, who are serving their punishment, to use their skills productively.

EFD OFFICER COBY SPEARS

Officer Coby Spears is a highly intelligent young man.

He attended the National Fire Academy's Managing Company Officer 2-week program. This class is a shortened version of the Executive Fire Officer class.

Students are chosen by their resume. Only a fraction of those who apply for the class are chosen.

Coby also attended a 1-week Refinery Fire Training class in Texas. The improved relationship with the refinery in El Dorado allowed us to send Coby with the El Dorado Refinery covering all the cost.

Coby also puts together the department's annual video showing all the accomplishments for the year.

TRAINING TOWER

The EFD got a new training tower at little cost to the El Dorado citizens.

The Butler Community College paid the entire cost of the structure.

The only cost to citizens was the cost of concrete and groundwork. That work was done by city crews.

A PRAYER FOR POLLY

She was a beautiful petite lady. A lifelong resident of El Dorado who worked her entire life -starting with her first job that helped her parents through the depression, then Safeway, then the bank, and then middle school – until retiring in March. Her name was Polly.

You may not have known Polly, but if you asked any El Dorado firefighter you would discover they not only knew her, but they also loved her. And this is the story of why.

Several years ago, the firefighters got to know Polly when they began to see her every morning at the El Dorado YMCA. Polly was there walking with her friends – walking her daily two miles – and would always say "hello" to the firefighters. But that was just the beginning.

The "hellos" evolved into good old-fashioned ribbing and that transformed into hugs – daily hugs for all the firefighters.

But it didn't stop there. Polly then began bringing fruit, cookies, and candy for the firefighters. There- after, each firefighter received a card

on their birthday. Firefighters described the joy in Polly's eyes and her smile as something special.

A few months ago, Polly started having some joint pain and had to take some time off from the YMCA. Before she left, she gave one of the firefighters a stack of predated signed birthday cards that covered the rest of the year. What the firefighters didn't know was Polly had gotten some bad news from her doctor. She had a rare aggressive cancer that was attacking her kidneys.

Firefighters heard the news of her illness and that she had moved in with her son. So, they rallied the troops for visits – with multiple arrangements of flowers and love.

During one of those visits Polly was asked how she managed the expense of all the cooking, the fruit, and the cards. She replied, "if you want to do something special for someone, you will find the means to do it." She said that she loved baking for the firefighters.

Polly was asked about her special secret – the secret of how she can bring such happiness to others. She downplayed the question saying, just be friendly. Help somebody that needs help."

Unfortunately, Polly only lived a short time afterwards. Firefighters each placed a yellow rose beside her ashes' box at her church service. Inlaid in the top of it was a St. Florian medal – the Patron Saint of firefighters, given to her by me, the Fire Chief.

EFD STAIRWAY CLIMB – 911 REMEMBRANCE

They came to Wichita from multiple departments across the State of Kansas. Some cities had great representation, and some not so great. The City of El Dorado was in the great category. El Dorado sent ten

MY CAREER IN ELDORADO

firefighters to participate in Wichita's first annual 911 Stairway Climb. Participants per ratio of populace put El Dorado at the top.

The climb was one hundred ten floors in the Epic Center. Five- and one-half trips up the 20-story building were required. A representation of the one hundred ten floors of the Twin Towers in New York City. Lest we never forget. The event kicked off with a check-in of those coming to climb. Then a Pastor said a few words. Then the bagpipers and drummers played some music. And then it was time to climb.

Have you ever climbed 119 stories? If you haven't then you couldn't possibly know how difficult it is – especially with the firefighters wearing the added weight of coats, pants, and air packs. I was mighty proud of the El Dorado Firefighters.

PAWS FOR PREVENTION - HALLOWEEN

The El Dorado businessman decided to celebrate Halloween with an elaborate costume scarier than any movie character. He was a big, dark green monster.

His clothes were shredded like he had been mauled by a pack of pit bulls. And the mask – the right eye hung out and the left was embedded with an ice pick. "Mike the Monster" was a crowd favorite.

Everywhere he went folks gasped and giggled with fright. It would be a night that Mike would long remember. Unfortunately, it wouldn't be a fun memory.

"Mike the Monster" decided to cross a busy highway later that evening. His vision through the scary mask was limited. Likewise, the dark costume was practically invisible to the car driver. The monster was struck at 40 mph.

Hollywood monsters might be invincible, but humans dressed as monsters aren't. Mike was lucky that he survived, but his serious injuries would remind him of Halloween night forever.

So, what is the point of telling you this story? There are hundreds, possibly thousands, of stories like Mike's – some with sadder endings.

What if we learned from their stories?

What if we thought about Mike when we chose our costume? What if we thought about Mike before crossing a busy street? Costumes can be fun without being dangerous.

And if we are on the topic of Halloween Safety let's include a few additional things:

- Pick a non-flammable costume.
- Carry a flashlight or a glow stick.
- Take off your mask when walking between houses.
- Never go into a person's home you don't know.

Here is a link to more information (Halloween-safety.com). Educate yourself so you don't suffer a terrible injury like "Mike the Monster."

PLANES: FIRE & RESCUE

As the children exited the Cinema 6 "Planes: Fire & Rescue" movie they were greeted by El Dorado firefighters. In addition to visiting the movie, firefighters had fire safety goody bags to give the children.

Cox Communication Store Manager Leah Ford was one of those families who attended the movie with her children. She also did something special besides going to the movie (which she said would've been a Wichita trip if not for the firefighters).

Yesterday, Leah read the story about the El Dorado firefighters at Cinema 6 today. So, she put out an Internet challenge.

Fire departments nation-wide were challenged to greet "Planes: Fire & Rescue" movie goers too. So, how did it go? Leah heard from one fire department that's a fair distance from Kansas – Galveston, Texas!

Thank you, Disney. Thank you, children. Thank you, firefighters.

NEW SAW DONATED

EFD FF Derrick Boggs along with the businessman who donated the funds for the saw's purchase.

I found businessmen in each of the communities of the four departments I served that were generous in providing funds for fire department needs.

All you needed to do was ask.

TOWER 1

Dating back as far as one can look is the practice of christening a new fire truck. The very first fire trucks were horse drawn and many of the streets were made of dirt. As a matter of fact, the City of El Dorado had two horses named Ned and Ted, which we have a custom-made decal on Tower 1 depicting them.

Firefighters also have a long tradition of keeping their fir ae trucks polished clean. So, the trucks are washed before they are pulled back into the fire station after a call for service making them ready for call.

Children and some adults came forward and helped christen Tower 1 by washing it down.

I asked for everyone's attention. I then asked everybody to bow their heads while I said the blessing for Tower 1.

BLESS THIS TRUCK
Lord, the emergencies there will be many.
Often this truck and those who ride it will be in harm's way. Father,
bless this truck and the men and women who man it.
Protect it and protect them while they protect others.
All this we ask humbly of you.
Amen

Tower 1 was the result of a commitment from a City Manager and City Commissioners to purchase a million-dollar truck. It was also the result of many hours of work from a truck committee of dedicated LFD personnel.

MY TWO SONS – MATT AND WESTON

The fire service is notorious for having systems where sons of firefighters follow along in their father's footsteps, within the same department.

There's nothing that would make me prouder than having one of my sons, Matt or Weston, do just that. Both are physically fit to a high level.

When I was the Deputy Chief in Salina, Matt would often ride along with me during the afterhours.

But neither of my sons ever took a fancy to following in father's footsteps as a career.

I think where we may fall short in careers, is we don't learn from the different principles of many careers.

Both of my sons competed in sports and there's no doubt that both learned some valuable lessons from doing so. Those lessons would've helped them in a fire service job. Some of the Coaches that coached my boys were Ed Nave, Tim Buyse, Mike Garritson, Chris Meis, Harold Bechard.

The media was another learning experience my sons learned from ways I partnered with the media, Matt is a marketing specialist and co-owns a professional fitness center along with Weston. It's

named"The Dub". They train young boys and girls from across the United States.

The media is an important feature of their business,

My son Weston is a head high school football coach.

I believe both marketing and coaching have areas where one can learn things that would help you

with a career in the fire service.

I'm super proud of both my sons for the success they have had as businessmen and fathers.

NFA ATTENDANCE – LEADERSHIP PICTURE

During my tenure we were able to send 6 firefighters to the National Fire Academy in Emmitsburg, Maryland.

The NFA training for firefighters is the premier of any available anywhere. The training covers the whole gamut of firefighter training.

The NFA has a great group of leadership courses. To the side is a Chad picture that says Leadership without words. The picture was used for a Leadership article in the Fire Chief magazine.

CHAPTER 6
A SUMMARY WITH AN ENDING

THE STORY OF MY LIFE

I started work as an FF firefighter with the SFD Salina Fire Department in 1978. The pay I received was minimum wage. With such a low salary, FFs had to work secondary jobs to make ends meet. Employee turnover was high. If you were stationed at a substation, you might never meet a new FF before they left, taking another job that paid better.

When responding to fires, FFs stood on the tailboard of the fire truck, hanging on to a chest high cross bar. FF attire consisted of a helmet, bare skin face/ neck (no face-hood), cotton hardware gloves, and a thigh-length coat that came down over rubber boots that were pulled up to the crotch area.

Air packs were a 15-minute sling style that rested across the FFs chest. The air- packs were only worn on large interior fires. In the first 2 months of Steve working at the SFD, there were two major fires – the Larson Lumber Yard fire and the St. John Military School fire. Both fires resulted in complete loss of the structures.

The pay was poor, and equipment and trucks were also poor. But a month after I started, Dave Robertson was hired as the new SFD fire chief. Robertson and new city manager Rufus Nye made immediate improvements at the department. The department also had funds for training, for those firefighters willing to go. I took advantage of the opportunities.

I became one of the first group of SFD FFs to become EMT Emergency Medical Technicians. This was before the ambulance operations were run by the SFD.

Many of the SFD FFs were smokers when Steve came on the department in 1978. There were no restrictions for where you could "light up." Television room, dining room, bedroom, everywhere. I found out about a New England Medical study citing the health danger to not only those smoking, but also to non-smokers from second-hand smoke. Steve wrote a petition to banish smoking in the fire house and he got many of the FFs signatures on it. The petition was sent to Chief Robertson who passed the petition. This was years before the City of Salina placed smoking restrictions on city buildings.

I became a fire engineer in 1984 and one of 3 SFD FFs to take paramedic training in 1985, when the SFD took over ambulance operations. The group had to drive to Hutchinson, KS 3 nights a week to take the year-long training.

In 1986 I went to a week-long FF physical fitness program in Dallas, TX. Part of the training was called the "Combat Challenge." The combat challenge was a multi-station course that had to be completed in an established time. The combat challenge was the beginning of a further broadened fitness program through Salina Family Physicians, run by fitness expert Adrienne Gapner. She is still serving the department.

I became an EMS Lt. in 1988, a new position overseeing the ambulance operations for the shift. I loved taking care of people with EMS operations, but I had a life-long goal of becoming a fire chief. I knew I needed more experience in fire operations. So, in 1993 I took the promotional process for fire lieutenant and finished first to fill an opening.

In 1993 myself and paramedic Greg Brockway produced a book on the history of the SFD. We did research at the Salina Public Library plus interviews with retirees. I wrote the book with assistance from high school English school teacher Bev Davis. Greg did the photography work. The book was produced by Jostin's book production company.

I served as one of three Union 782 officers, the other two were Willis Sutton and Rick Nicholson.

In 1996 I was promoted to the position of Deputy Chief.

I continued to take additional training opportunities. I took night courses to finish my bachelor's degree through Kansas State University. I became a hazardous material technician when the SFD took on hazardous material response. I became certified as fire officer 1 and 2, went through the Leadership Salina program, and took the Kansas University Public Manager program.

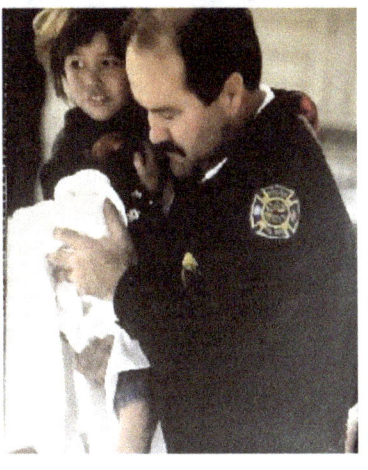

But the pinnacle of my training was in 2001 when I successfully finished the prestigious Executive Fire Officer program at the National Fire Academy in Emmitsburg, Maryland. Students attend 4 two-week leadership classes. After each class a college level research paper is reviewed by a college professor. A minimum score of 80% on all sections must be met. There are only a few EFO graduates in Kansas.

SFD fire chief Tom Girard retired in 2000 and I was named interim fire chief. One of the first things I did was start a bi-weekly newsletter covering department activities of all things going on so all FFs would be informed. An annual report was written using newsletter material.

In 2001 a promotional process for the selection of the SFD fire chief position was conducted with a nation-wide search. I was a participant but was not chosen. I stepped down to the deputy chief position.

After the World Trade Center terrorist attack that killed 343 emergency responders on September 11th, 2001, the city had a dedication to all police officers and firefighters. It was held at the Bicentennial Center. I wrote an honorary editorial that was posted in the Salina Journal that day. A professional video was shown as the capstone to the event. The video concludes with a Salina Journal photographer Tom Dorsey picture of myself carrying a small soot-faced child that was one of three children involved in a house fire. The fire claimed the life of one of the children.

I finished my 28 years with the SFD in 2006 when I accepted the fire chief position with the City of Leavenworth, KS. I loved the City of Salina, but my career goal was fire chief, and this was a great opportunity to lead the oldest fire department in KS.

Upon my arrival in Leavenworth, I found a fire department operating with a dysfunctional 2-shift platoon system versus a 3-shift system used by all other KS departments. I immediately worked with the administrative officers and prepared a detailed report for the city manager and city commissioners showing the need for a changeover. A department- wide meeting, including wives, was held to explain the need for the change. A full shift of new officers, engineers, and mechanics was part of the change.

The city manager and commissioners all voted in favor of the change. I immediately conducted promotional processes followed by

badge-pinning ceremonies with families invited. The FFs got to choose who they wanted to pin their badge.

New operating procedures were written, a medical director hired, training with the county ambulance personnel, new dual response procedures with the Fort Leavenworth fire department, a bi-weekly newsletter, an annual report, and an end of the year dinner with families was conducted. My wife Rosie prepared the meal.

Another successful accomplishment was the Halloween Fire Safety House – the brainchild of SFD public educator Deb Weaver and her husband Bill Weaver. The SFD put on the event for two years, but they decided to discontinue it. I requested from the SFD fire chief to borrow it, and he said yes. The event consisted of 5 rooms with lights, painted backdrops, music, and costumed actors. I got two additional rooms painted by 2 Kansas Prison inmates. Each of the rooms had a different fire safety message.

Deb and SFD fire lieutenant Willis Sutton came to Leavenworth and helped too.

The event was a hit with over 1,000 people going through the rooms. The 1,000 people loved it, the drama teacher and his students loved it, the firefighters who mingled with the crowd loved it, the Kansas City Chief's super fan came, and he loved it.

Letters from numerous dignitaries were received days after the event, including the city manager, the mayor, and the city commissioners.

I was happy with Leavenworth and loved the firefighters, but in 2009 I needed to retire because of financial pension reasons concerning payouts received when leaving Salina.

I still loved being a fire chief, so I took a job with Stafford County KS as the emergency service director, overseeing ambulance operations, fire operations, and emergency management operations. Two weeks before my start date, one of the firefighters suffered a fatal heart attack after fighting a grass land fire. I made the trip from Leavenworth to Stafford County twice, first to console the family and to make sure all documentation was done for the spouse to receive line of duty firefighter insurance benefits. The second trip was so I could attend the funeral, meet firefighters, and give a short heart-felt speech.

Most Stafford emergency responders are volunteers, and this brought me a new-found respect for those who do their emergency job without pay.

During my time in Stafford I got a new ambulance, new wildland fire trucks, a new fire station, a new training room/emergency operations center, new portable radios, ten thousand dollars annually from state emergency management funds, a new rescue truck with a full complement of hydraulic rescue tools donated by a local businessman, uniforms for the four paid personnel, a new command vehicle, a generator for the emergency operation's center, and another 20K portable generator from the State.

A blog was started to keep the entire county responders informed about what everyone throughout the county was doing. An annual report was written into professional produced books that were distributed to each responder at a family meal prepared by my wife Rosie. A video as the capstone to the night was shown with stories from the blog and pictures collected from St. John's News reporter/photographer Terry Spradley. I gave Terry a safety vest and a portable radio to assist him in getting the best emergency scene pictures possible. Terry was given a personal invite to the annual celebration. He was treated as a member of the team.

Overseeing all the county emergency operations kept me super busy and away from home a lot, but the rural life wasn't what brought happiness to my wife Rosie – there just wasn't much for her to do.

So, I took a small state pension from Stafford County and accepted the fire chief's job in Eldorado, KS.

While in Eldorado one of my officers said I changed the culture of the department. I think this was in no way meant as criticism of past chiefs. Every fire chief has a style of their own.

Other things that I did do was did do was sign on the first female fire science student, implemented the use of drones for training and incidents, FFs made 6 trips to TEEKs training at College Station, TX, made upgrades to FF gear, purchased a 100 ft. aerial platform tower, FFs made 5 trips to the National Fire Academy, had the Kansas State Prison inmates build an oak frame portrait case and picture frames, built a 3-story multipurpose training tower, updated the fire pup costume, raised $15K for MDA, improved relations with Butler County agencies, purchased a new chief command vehicle, conducted 6 promotional processes, purchased a new report management system, updated the standard operating procedures, updated thermal imaging cameras, implemented a community outreach blog, established a partnership with photographer Chad Wittenberg, purchased fire cam helmets, and purchased the first wildland CNS apparatus.

I also had an end of the year get together with the entire group – paid FFs, volunteer FFs, fire science FFs, and their families. Dinner was prepared by my wife Rosie.

THE ENDING

It started as occasional absentee seizures in Stafford County. It didn't happen often enough that it kept me from performing my job. I was almost performing at my peak when I left.

But when I went to be the Fire Chief in El Dorado, the symptoms started to become more serious. Severe anxiety started to take place. Sleepless nights with pacing the basement started to make it impossible to continue my job as Fire Chief.

I reluctantly put in my resignation. Equipment and personnel were prepared to go without me.

I'm proud that an internal fire chief was chosen at each of the departments I worked.

I was diagnosed as having the beginning stages of Parkinsons and LBD Lewy Body Dementia. LBD is the disease that took the life of the great Robin Williams. The disease is one that has terrible effects on the body. Depletion of complete muscle mass. Severe anxiety.

First, it's the extremities. Mainly the toes and then the complete feet go numb, followed by hands going numb. It's called neuropathy.

Oral sticky saliva flows like a river in the mouth. Full body skin covering, like sweat, but sticky, is constant with a need to scrub the entire body nightly.

There is full body throbbing, muscular pain, of what muscle is left. Complete body muscles are destroyed. Weight loss is extreme.

I took two trips to the hospital by ambulance after falling from hypotension and musculature loss. Damaged neurons in the brain send out false messages to the heart resulting in severe drops in blood pressure. Called orthoscopic hypotension is the name for it.

As of now I'm still at home.

Many choose suicide before the disease takes its final course. Robin Williams made that choice.

As of the publication of this book, I fight a strong fight, but know the disease is terminal. I understand the end can be soon.

I don't think I was shortchanged though. I lived a wonderful life – a great wife, two special sons, five incredible grandchildren, and a career like no other.

I can go to death knowing that I left a legacy that will live on. I have told "The Story of my Life" with this book.

A firefighter starts his career at the first year's badge pinning and reciting of the Fireman's Prayer. So, it only seems proper that I close the door on this book with the Fireman's Prayer. It is posted on the back cover of this book. Please say it for me.

Writing this book has brought me enjoyment. I hope that it provides you with enjoyment too.

Stay safe my friends!

ACKNOWLEDGEMENT

First and foremost, thanks to my wonderful wife Rosie. Without her I wouldn't have been able to pursue advancement in my career. First there were multiple night classes for certifications and educational degrees. I also spent 8 weeks in Emmittsburg, Maryland at the National Fire Academy. Rosie took care of our two sons and our household, by herself, during my time away.

Every single member of the four departments I served deserve recognition, but space and memory only allow me to list, and show, a few.

While in Salina, fire chief Tom Girard promoted me to Deputy Chief. I stepped into the role of Interim chief upon Tom's retirement. Administrative Assistant Judy Piercy provided organization for the department.

My career took another large step when I took the position of fire chief with Leavenworth, KS. Leavenworth Assistant Chief Mark was instrumental with several large-scale changes. Administrative Assistant Cary Collins was the key organizational specialist.

A SUMMARY WITH AN ENDING

The next career step was Stafford County KS. T.J. Rockenbach and Misty Blakeslee had major roles.

The last career step I had was ElDorado, KS. The key organization assistant was deputy chief Joe Haag, who was promoted to chief upon my departure.

Last, but not least, my oldest son Matthew took the responsibility of being the publisher for the book. Without his direction the book wouldn't have been possible.

First and foremost, thanks to my wonderful wife Rosie. Without her I wouldn't have been able to pursue advancement in my career. First there were multiple night classes for certifications and educational degrees. I also spent 8 weeks in Emmittsburg, Maryland at the National Fire Academy. Rosie took care of our two sons and our household, by herself, during my time away.

Every single member of the four departments I served deserve recognition, but space and memory only allow me to list, and show, a few.

While in Salina, fire chief Tom Girard promoted me to Deputy Chief. I stepped into the role of Interim chief upon Tom's retirement. Administrative Assistant Judy Piercy provided organization for the department.

My career took another large step when I took the position of fire chief with Leavenworth, KS. Leavenworth Assistant Chief Mark was instrumental with several large-scale changes. Administrative Assistant Cary Collins was the key organizational specialist.

The next career step was Stafford County KS. T.J. Rockenbach and Misty Blakeslee had major roles.

The last career step I had was ElDorado, KS. The key organization assistant was deputy chief Joe Haag, who was promoted to chief upon my departure.

Last, but not least, my oldest son Matthew took the responsibility of being the publisher for the book. Without his direction the book wouldn't have been possible.

First and foremost, thanks to my wonderful wife Rosie. Without her I wouldn't have been able to pursue advancement in my career. First there were multiple night classes for certifications and educational degrees. I also spent 8 weeks in Emmittsburg, Maryland at the National Fire Academy. Rosie took care of our two sons and our household, by herself, during my time away.

Every single member of the four departments I served deserve recognition, but space and memory only allow me to list, and show, a few.

While in Salina, fire chief Tom Girard promoted me to Deputy Chief. I stepped into the role of Interim chief upon Tom's retirement. Administrative Assistant Judy Piercy provided organization for the department.

My career took another large step when I took the position of fire chief with Leavenworth, KS. Leavenworth Assistant Chief Mark was instrumental with several large-scale changes. Administrative Assistant Cary Collins was the key organizational specialist.

The next career step was Stafford County KS. T.J. Rockenbach and Misty Blakeslee had major roles.

The last career step I had was ElDorado, KS. The key organization assistant was deputy chief Joe Haag, who was promoted to chief upon my departure.

Last, but not least, my oldest son Matthew took the responsibility of being the publisher for the book. Without his direction the book wouldn't have been possible.

ACKNOWLEDGEMENT

First and foremost, thanks to my wonderful wife Rosie. Without her I wouldn't have been able to pursue advancement in my career. First there were multiple night classes for certifications and educational degrees. I also spent 8 weeks in Emmittsburg, Maryland at the National Fire Academy – 4 two-week sessions. Rosie took care of our two sons and our household, by herself, during my time away.

Every single member of the four departments I served deserve recognition, but space and memory only allow me to list, and show, a few.

While in Salina, fire chief Tom Girard promoted me to Deputy Chief. I stepped into the role of Interim chief upon Tom's retirement. Administrative Assistant Judy Piercy provided organization for the department.

My career took another large step when I took the position of fire chief with Leavenworth, KS. Leavenworth Assistant Chief Mark was instrumental with several large-scale changes. Administrative Assistant Cary Collins was the key organizational specialist.

The next career step was Stafford County KS. T.J. Rockenbach and Misty Blakeslee had major roles while I was there.

The last career step I had was ElDorado, KS. The key organization assistant was deputy chief Joe Haag, who was promoted to chief upon my departure.

Last, but not least, my oldest son Matthew took the responsibility of being the publisher for the book. Without his direction the book wouldn't have been possible.

PHOTOS

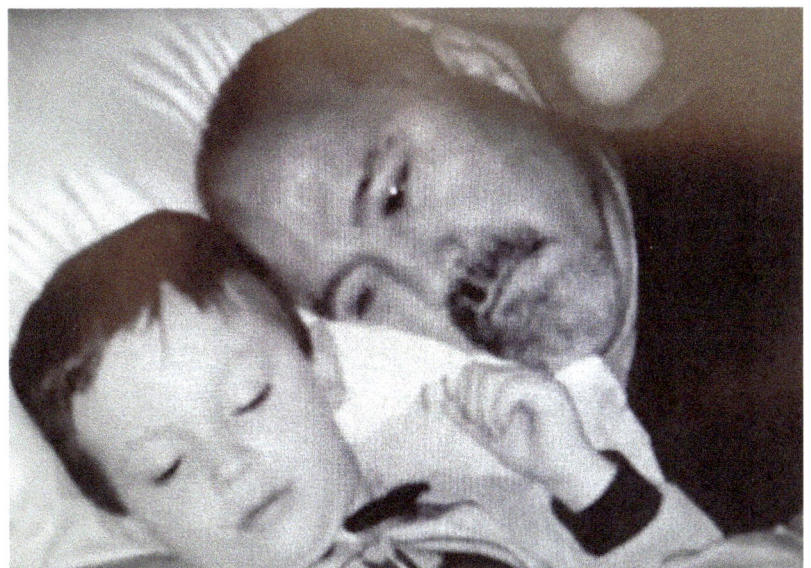

ACKNOWLEDGEMENT

ACKNOWLEDGEMENT

THE STORY OF MY LIFE

"I've been waiting for a chance like that since I've been here. I knew I had to do something with it."
— Fort Hays State University sophomore pitcher Matt Moody

ABOVE: Fort Hays State University players celebrate after their 16-3 victory over University of Southern Colorado Saturday at Larks Park. The win gave the Tigers the Rocky Mountain Athletic Conference tournament championship. BELOW: Tiger junior Cam Houston watches his home run in the sixth inning.

Tigers make for 'Moody' champs

Pitcher helps Fort Hays take RMAC championship

By NICK SCHWIEN
Hays Daily News

Matt Moody didn't know he was going to be given a chance to pitch in one of the biggest games of his life.

That is, until 30 minutes before it started.

But it didn't distract the sophomore right-handed pitcher on the Fort Hays State University baseball team.

"I found out about 30 minutes before the game," Moody said.

"Coach said they were going to talk it over and see who was going to go. They came back and told me I was going to get the start. It was pretty exciting."

And all Moody did was pitch the Tigers to their first title at the Rocky Mountain Athletic Conference Championships since 1996 with a convincing 16-3 win over University of Southern Colorado Saturday at Larks Park. FHSU won the first title game earlier Saturday, 9-4, over the Thunderwolves to force a second game. The two wins helped the Tigers secure a spot in next week's NCAA Division II West Region Championships, barring some type of unfortunate event.

Moody had pitched only 149 innings this season before Saturday. But when junior Nick VanBibber injured his shoulder warming up in the bullpen during the first game, the Tigers were left looking for a starter in the deciding game.

And Moody, a former standout at Salina South High School, got the nod for his first start of the season.

"I had no idea I was going to get that opportunity," he said. "I've been waiting for a chance like that since I've been here. I knew I had to do something with it."

That's just what the sophomore did. And in the process, he did something the rest of the FHSU pitching staff had trouble doing in previous games against USC — shut the Thunderwolves down.

"We knew we had the best guy out there for the right job ... Matt Moody," said senior relief pitcher Ben Ford.

● CHAMPS / SEE PAGE B2

ACKNOWLEDGEMENT

Annie Wolfe | The Times
Grant Larson works on his swing using the HitTrax system at the Wamego Sports Academy. Inset: Weston Moody, Dusti Gallagher and Matt Moody are the owners of the Academy (not pictured, co-owner Paul Gallagher).

Wamego Sports Academy owners dream big

Annie Wolfe
The Times

The temperatures may be frigid, but the season for America's pastime is right around the corner and Wamego Sports Academy has opened just in time for some indoor preseason training.

When the opportunity to own an indoor baseball/softball training facility presented itself, Paul and Dusti Gallagher and brothers Matt and Weston Moody all had the same thought; it was the right thing at the right time.

"Paul and I had been thinking about this for a number of years," said Dusti. The Gallagher family has a passion for baseball and softball, with teenagers Nate and Maya playing from the time they could hold a bat.

Matt Moody voiced a similar sentiment, "the idea was that we'd always have a facility somewhere."

Matt and Weston Moody both had the opportunity to play baseball at Fort Hays State University.

With a shared desire to offer young athletes more training opportunities, it only made sense for the four to come together

Please see
Sports Academy PG. A8

ACKNOWLEDGEMENT

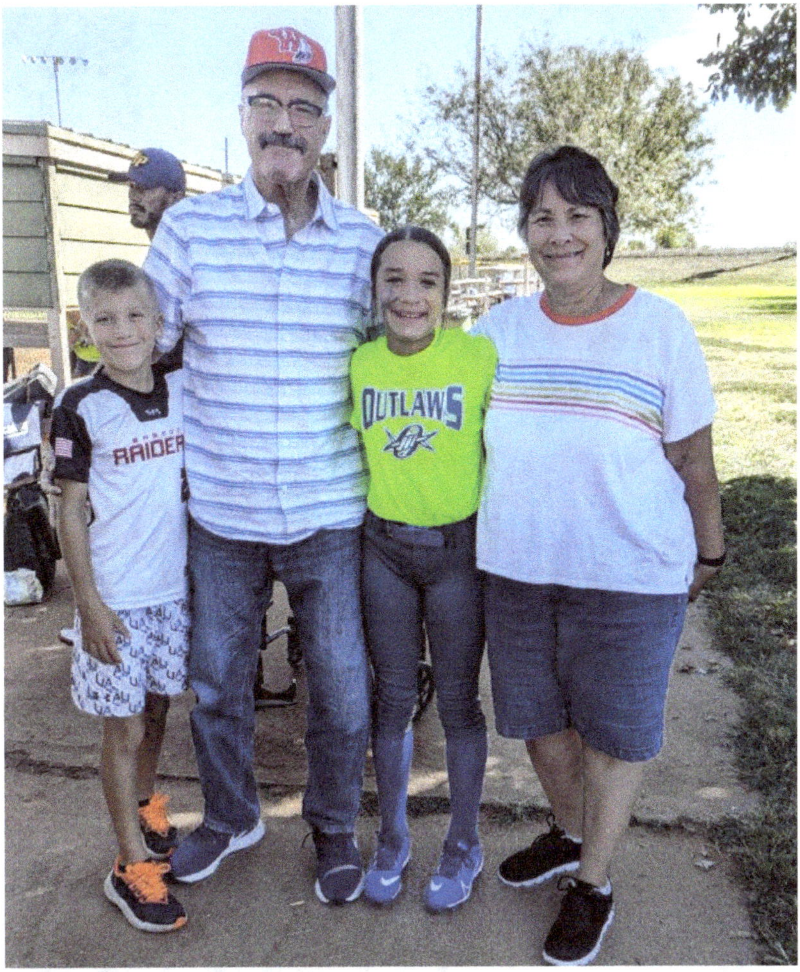
RAIDER
OUTLAWS

EL DORADO
KANSAS WILDFIRES
BATTLING FIRES & FATIGUE
BUTLER COUNTY
KWCH 12 HD
10:00 52°

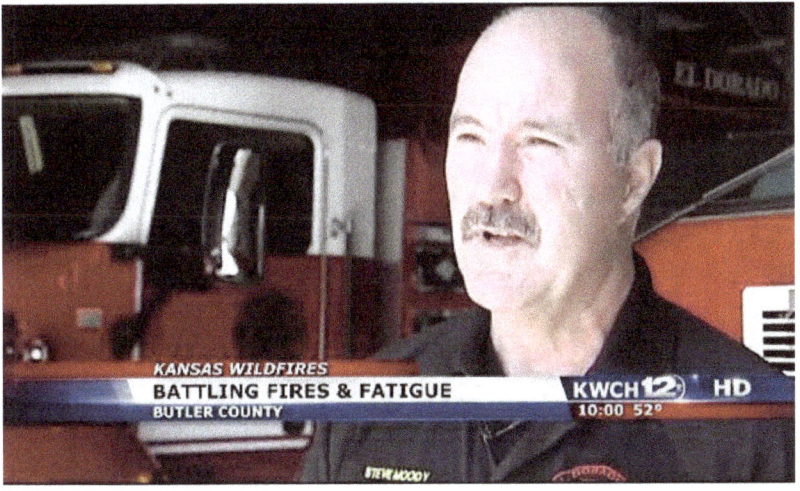

ACKNOWLEDGEMENT

ACKNOWLEDGEMENT